WHAT MAKES PERSUASIVE SALES COPY PERSUASIVE

COVETED SECRETS REVEALED!

RUSSELL J. MARTINO

Copyright © 2017 Russell J. Martino

All rights reserved. No part of this publication may be reproduced, distributed, or transmitted in any form or by any means, including photocopying, recording, or other electronic or mechanical methods, without the prior written permission of the publisher, except in the case of brief quotations embodied in critical reviews and certain other noncommercial uses permitted by copyright law.

Book cover design and layout and interior formatting by, Ellie Bockert Augsburger of Creative Digital Studios. www.CreativeDigitalStudios.com

Cover design features:
Lightbulb Idea: © Kenishirotie / Adobe Stock

ACKNOWLEDGEMENTS

We all stand on the shoulders of giants.

The giants in marketing, sales and copywriting who have influenced me the most by reading their books over and over again, studying their sales letters with an intensity some say boarders on madness, and in some cases, being personally mentored by include;

John E. Kennedy, Robert Collier, Claude C. Hopkins, John Caples, Eugene Schwartz, Rosser Reeves, David Ogilvy, Elmo Wheeler, Zig Ziglar, Gary Halbert, Gary Bencivenga, Jay Abraham, Dan Kennedy and Clayton Makepeace.

These men paved the road all successful marketers and copywriters travel today.

With every win I produce for a client, I thank them – and study their work even more.

TABLE OF CONTENTS

Preface: Your Turning Point 1

FOREWORD: How Kryptonite Saved Superman 7

What Makes Persuasive Sales Copy – Persuasive... Coveted Secrets Revealed! 16

The Fortune Not Made On Business Not Done Is Real... 86

The Most Powerful Selling Tool on Earth... And How To Use It To Grow Your Business 99

The Right Message For Your Business What It Sounds Like - What's Your Alternative Is Getting It Right Worth the Effort 109

Secrets of Pixel Marketing Revealed 132

Converting Copy into Cash A Special Report... 139

A message for you from the author 148

PREFACE
YOUR TURNING POINT

Imagine doubling your sales over the next year. What would that mean for you and your family? What would that mean for your bank account?

The information in this short book gives you that power.

Here's what you need to know...

Once upon a time, if you were willing to work hard, be friendly and advertise – you could start a business and do well. But all that has changed.

Today competition is fierce.

The noise in the market place is deafening. With more and more businesses competing for attention, we have become experts at ignoring sales messages.

With all the noise, marketing that once worked well, work less and less.

To make matters worse...

With so many people trying to sell so many things, your prospects are slammed with hundreds of sales messages every day. *Junk mail, TV and radio ads, banner ads, pop-ups, bill boards, newspapers, magazines* – these messages are everywhere.

Sales messages are so abundant, most people, including most of your prospects, instantly dismiss all advertising as junk. They toss your precious brochures in the trash without a second glance. They ignore your messages, delete your emails. And pay someone to screen their mail, screen their calls, protect their time... and keep sales people away.

With more and more sales messages vying for your prospects attention, plus the fact that most people hate being 'sold' - and are quick to trash anything that looks like advertising - your job of connecting with your prospects – having your sales message consumed - and getting your prospect to *WANT* your product or service, is more challenging than ever.

SO WHAT'S IT TAKE TO STAND OUT IN A CROWDED MARKETPLACE? HOW DO YOU GET PEOPLE TO WANT TO DO BUSINESS WITH YOU?

You GET your prospects' attention by appealing to their curiosity or self-interest.

You HOLD their attention by making your message about something important to them.

And you SELL by delivering a message persuasive enough to answer questions. Handle objections. And get your prospect excited about doing business with you.

- Only then will you be noticed
- Only then will your message hit home.
- Only then will your prospects *have reason to respond to your message*. Call you direct. Visit you online. Accept your call. And do business with you.

But crafting the right message is just part of the challenge.

You have more ways to reach people than ever.

Besides print, direct mail, radio and television, the Internet gives you dozens, if not hundreds, of new ways to spend money and time trying to reach people.

Social media, Facebook ads, Google Ad Words, organic search, LinkedIn, Pinterest, eBooks, banner ads, product launches, email marketing, funnels, blog posts, newsletters, joint ventures, pod casts – this is just the tip of the iceberg.

Your choices are dizzying!

But the fact remains...

You can do all this and a bag of chips - and still not sell a thing. Because until you reach the RIGHT PROSPECTS with the RIGHT MESSAGE - that gets attention, holds interest and is persuasive enough to convert lookers into buyers, nothing else matters, because nothing else happens.

WANT TO SELL MORE?

Whether your product costs ten cents, or a hundred and fifty thousand dollars, THE KEY TO SELL MORE is TRAFFIC and CONVERSION. That's it.

Without reaching enough of the right people, you speak to an empty auditorium.

And without the right message - the auditorium may as well stay empty for all the good it will do you. People don't buy because you show up.

THE MAGIC IS IN THE MESSAGE

Without a unique message to distinguish you from every Johnny-Come-Lately waving hands in your prospects face trying to sell something, you sound like anyone on any street corner hawking wares, shouting *'buy from me because I want you to buy from me'*.

- Selling is not about waving arms, slick brochures or cool tag lines.
- Selling is not even about products or services.
- Selling is about human nature.

Selling is about connecting with people – about delivering a message so *'on the mark'*, your prospects are happy to receive the message. And are excited to respond.

Selling is about CONSISTENTLY getting the RIGHT MESSAGE to the RIGHT PEOPLE.

Without the RIGHT MESSAGE reaching THE RIGHT PEOPLE ... you have nothing.

> Developing messages that connect with prospects and move them to act, so they take the next step and contact you, accept your call – or just buy - is what DIRECT RESPONSE COPYWRITING & DIRECT RESPONSE MARKETING are all about.

Einstein said, "Nothing happens until something moves."

The RIGHT DIRECT RESPONSE MARKETING STRATEGY *gets things moving,* because the right strategy keeps you in front of an endless supply of good prospects who may benefit greatly from your product or service.

The RIGHT DIRECT RESPONSE MESSAGE *keeps things moving,* because the right message gets attention, engages prospects, holds attention, and converts lookers into buyers... so *the cash register rings!*

And that's what this book is all about... ringing the cash register, increasing your sales to all new levels, you earning more profit than ever - *and finally getting the kind of payoff you deserve for all the blood, sweat and tears you pour into your business.*

WHAT MAKES PERSUASIVE SALES COPY – PERSUASIVE

HERE'S WHAT I'VE GOT FOR YOU...

PART 1: WHAT MAKES PERSUASIVE SALES COPY – PERSUASIVE

If your goal is to persuade in print, this is the mother lode. These are the coveted secrets of *what makes persuasive copy PERSUASIVE.* Apply them in your copy, and you will sell more. Enjoy higher profits. And feel better about life, the universe and everything.

Perhaps more importantly, with these secrets at your command...

You will be able to read a marketing copywriters' work and objectively know IF their copy is persuasive, WHY it is persuasive or WHY it is not persuasive if it fails the test.

And you will know all this BEFORE you hire them to write copy that will determine your sales revenue and profitability.

Not one business owner in a thousand has this skill. Knowing this gives you a tremendous building-building, profit-growing, sales-increasing advantage.

PART 2: MINDSET OF A DIRECT MARKETING ENTREPRENEUR

In Chapter two, The Fortune Not Made on Business Not Done, we examine the tremendous cost of delivering the wrong message to your prospects. And you see how simply replacing a weak sales message with a stronger one can multiple your sales many times without you spending an extra dime on advertising.

If all you do is read this chapter and apply the ideas in your business, don't be surprised if your sales double over the next year.

In Chapter three, we explore The Right Message For Your Business.

The RIGHT MESSAGE scribbled in Crayola... will out sell the wrong message printed on a slick brochure designed by an award-winning graphics team... every single time. *Everything you need to know is here for you in this chapter.*

In Chapter four, Your Most Powerful Sales Tool, I take you behind the scenes and show you step-by-step how a new company went from no sales - to over $200-million in sales in just eighteen short months.

More importantly, you see how you can apply the same strategy to double or maybe even triple your sales over a short time.

Read this chapter carefully. Put the ideas to work in your business. And this book may be worth over a million dollars to you in the next year alone.

PART 3: SELL MORE. START NOW. HERE'S HOW.

In Chapter five, What It Takes To Transform Your Business Into An High-Powered Wealth-Building Money-Making Machine

BONUS REPORTS

Secrets of Pixel Marketing Revealed – *How to Get Your Sales Message In Front of Thousands of Good Prospects Every Week For Pennies Each...* by Brian Hahn, founder and CEO of GoSocialExperts.com

Converting Copy Into Cash – What professionals who work by appointment, coaches, consultants and speakers need to know to build a big business fast – by Parthiv Shah, co-founder of eLaunchers.com one of Americas' fastest growing digital marketing agencies.

FOREWORD
HOW KRYPTONITE SAVED SUPERMAN

> "As soon as you move one step up from the bottom, your effectiveness depends on your ability to reach others through the spoken and written word." - Peter Drucker

WHEN SUPERMAN BEGAN THE STORY HAD A PROBLEM.

Superman was invincible. All powerful. He could not be harmed. Holding readers interest in a Superhero with no weakness, no flaws and no way to be harmed, injured or even threatened was a challenge.Since Superman was guaranteed to win every conflict, every time, no matter what ... it didn't take long for people to get bored and for sales to drop. New episode. Superman wins. The end.

Before dumping the series, which was a consideration, the writers decided to give Superman a challenge he couldn't leap over in a single bound. They did that by making him vulnerable to something powerful enough to injure or even kill the man of steel. That vulnerability was to Kryptonite. Just being around it drained Superman's power. A bad guy with Kryptonite, available on earth thanks to meteor showers, could stop, injure, imprison or even kill Superman.

With the addition of a deadly threat, Superman winning was no longer guaranteed. Bad guys could wield real power. The story became more interesting. And sales began to soar. With Kryptonite in the story, Superman is more like you and me. Working hard to keep the forces of darkness at bay. And doing his best to stay alert so you don't get hijacked, dowsed with Kryptonite. And kicked to the curb before you even know what hit you. Superman comics went on to become so popular, most people in the Western World recognize Kryptonite as a reference to something that can do you great harm. Had the writers not adapted, had they not given readers what they want, had they stubbornly insisted on doing it *their way,* had they not invented Kryptonite...

The Superman series would have died. Great stories would have never been told. And a franchise worth billions would have been kicked to the curb and forgotten.

MEET THE REAL MASTERS OF THE UNIVERSE

Jerry Seinfeld pointed out, (accurately I believe), that males don't see heroes like Superman, Batman, Iron Man, and Captain America as comic book characters.

We see them as career choices.

In my thirty plus years-experience helping business owners sell expensive products and services, newsletters, high-dollar investment opportunity and more, I'd say Seinfeld is spot-on. Most business owners see themselves as 'master of the universe'. At least the master of THEIR universe ... the one who shows up every day ... the one who solves problems ... the one who knows more than all others about your customers, products, the market, the competition, what can or can't be done in your business, the best way to sell your product or service. And so on.

The master-of-the-universe mentality can be both good and bad.

On one hand, somebody has to take responsibility. And who better to take charge and get things done in your business than you? The answer is, probably no one.

THE KRYPTONITE MIND-SET...

On the other hand, if you're a Master of the Universe type, it's easy to get locked into a limiting
mindset that stifles ideas, is out of touch with reality and blinds you to opportunity that could lead to your best most profitable years ever in business.

Buggy makers, *masters of their universe all,* failed to recognize, (or acknowledge), the catastrophic impact change would have on their business. As such, they failed to adapt to the changing environment. And with the arrival of the automobile - died a slow, painful deathBook stores failed to adapt to the changing environment brought on by digital technology. By not adapting, brick and mortar book stores have all but vanished since the arrival of Amazon.

Dentists who fail to adapt to the changing environment are being squashed by big-box dentistry chains, forced to work longer, earn less, downsize and put off retirement.

No business and no business owner is exempt.

Doctors, lawyers, financial professionals, manufacturers, retailers, service providers, all brick and mortar business owners, and anyone who sells anything that costs from a one-dollar to a million online or off is affected. If you own a business, this applies to YOU.

Your environment is changing at hyper-speed.

Web technology is more powerful and less expensive than ever. And while most business owners haven't fully harnessed the customer-securing, business-building power of this technology yet... With the right technology, you can reach more good prospects and tell your story more often in a single day than a team of salespeople could reach in a month without it. And with the right message, you can sell more of your product or service than ever.

With the right message – and the right technology to reach your prospects, deliver a powerful, engaging message and follow-up automatically, there's no limit to what you can do. This expands your reach. Expands your impact. And gives you massive potential selling power. This is where smart business is going. The advantages are too great to ignore. But if you ignore this, because *(like buggy-makers)* as master of your universe you know it won't work for your business, you know it won't work with your customers, you think you don't need it, or it's just not necessary, then by all means, be scared.

Be very scared!

Not because you can't live without the technology or the messaging it takes to get the job done. *After all, you've come this far without it. So why bother now?*

Be scared because right now, as you read these words, your competitors are working on it.

And when they get the message and the technology right, *which doesn't always happen the first time around,* and enter the market with the ability grab customers at will, they will outsell anyone without the same advantage. And you can kiss your market share and your profits goodbye.

Technology is just one example of massive environmental changes you face today.

YOUR PROSPECTS ARE BETTER INFORMED & MORE RESISTANT TO SALES MESSAGES THAN EVER.

It's a buyers' world pure and simple!

We fast-forward through commercials. Block pop-ups. Delete Spam at light speed. Screen calls with caller ID. Click out of online video or print sales message the second you lose interest.

WHAT MAKES PERSUASIVE SALES COPY - PERSUASIVE

And we are experts at ignoring all marketing or advertising messages we don't care to see.In other words ... *unless a message is so interesting you WANT to watch it, hear it or read it,* advertisers have no way to get and hold your attention long enough to sell anything.

This is a huge environmental change that has been developing for years.

Technology empowers this change. But the change is not about technology. It's about human nature.

Technology gives you the ability to deliver messages. That's it. And with the Internet, social media, email, Facebook, YouTube and a thousand other ways to get messages...

Your prospects; 1) have near unlimited things to pay attention to; 2) they have the ability to pay attention to WHAT EVER THEY WANT; and; 3) like you, they are able to filter out or instantly dismiss anything they are not interested in or don't want to be bothered with.

Online technology, including email, Web sites, social media, and so on... is like the U.S. Postal Service, UPS or Federal Express. The technology gives you the ability to DELIVER A MESSAGE.

But you don't respond to the digital message-delivery truck. You respond to the MESSAGE. And this is why getting the message right is so important. Without that you have nothing.

You can spend a fortune on technology. You can spend a zillion dollars on traffic. But unless your

messages; 1) reach the right people; 2) attract and hold their interest, and; 3) get your prospect excited about what you can do for THEM...

Your messages are ignored, just like you ignore anything that doesn't interest you, or give you GOOD reason to watch, read, download, reply, opt-in, sign-up, click, call or come by.

Species that fail to adapt to a changing environment die. They go extinct. Cease to exist. The lights go out. The doors close. Game over.

Thankfully you have a choice.

AVOID THE KRYPTONITE KILL-SHOT...

The Kryptonite Kill-Shot is evaluating your business through the *I-know-everything* belief

system. Then acting based on that belief and dismissing anything that doesn't validate what you think you know or agree with your view of how business should be done.

The master-of-the-universe mindset is like sirens whispering in Ulysses' ear, filling your head with bad ideas that sound good, luring you to sail your ship full speed ahead straight into the rocky shallows.

Yes of course you're right. You know best. Do it your way. That's ridiculous. It costs too much. It'll never work in your business. Sure sales are down and competition is tough, but so what, just work a little harder. Do what you've always done. You don't need that. You'll be fine. Don't change a thing.

If you experience this, don't feel bad. We all do. The problem is not having the thoughts.

The problem is being seduced by them - and not being open to strategic business-building ideas that harness the power of new technology. The problem is not crafting a powerful sales argument and not wielding the power of persuasive copywriting. The problem is believing your business is different and this 'stuff' just won't work.

Everyone has a comfort zone. And no one is excited about leaving it.

Everyone thinks they know best, especially about their business. And no one likes to be wrong.

But this is not about being right or wrong. This is about a business environment that has changed so much, business owners who fail to adapt... *are being left behind.*

This is about a technology and a type or messaging that until recently was out of reach for virtually all small business owners - and now is in reach - and already helping many have their best years ever.

In short, the environment has changed.

Business owners who adapt the technology AND GET THE MESSAGING RIGHT *will become the dominant businesses of their type in their market area.*

They will take customers, clients, patients or patrons from more established businesses who fail to adapt - as easy as a pro boxer in his prime could punch out a four-year old.

While *masters of the universe* who fail to adapt will work harder, earn less. And wonder why...

Business owners willing to leave their comfort zone, develop a strategic plan to grow, embrace the technology and commit to developing strong messaging and copywriting assets that connect with and persuade prospects... will dominate every market they enter.

If you ignore this... and your competitor seizes the opportunity, you'll lose market share, and your competitors will become the dominant force in a market that may have easily been yours.

> Trying to maintain market share or grow your business without those tools, *while competing against competitors who have them* - is like a guy with a teaspoon trying to dig a foundation for a hundred-story building, competing against a competitor using a dozen giant cranes. *Guess who wins.*

THE CURSE OF COMMON KNOWLEDGE...

> "It ain't what you don't know that gets you into trouble. It's what you know for sure that just ain't so." - Samuel Clemens

If you do something the way you've always done it because it's common knowledge, or because that's just how it's done in your industry, it's time to reevaluate and here's why.

Mediocrity is common. Exceptional, high-profit businesses are rare. And times are changing.

So unless your goal is to have a mediocre business with mediocre income and mediocre prospects for the future, flush the idea of doing the same old things the same old ways because it's 'common knowledge' or 'standard practice' right out of your mind.

Follow the crowd and you risk following the Pied Piper's rats straight off the cliff.

If you want more prospects, more sales and consistent growth you can count on...

If you want to leave competitors in the dust and have customers, clients, patients or patrons

standing in line ready to do business and excited about doing business with you...

Set the status quo aside.

If you need expertise you don't have... call in experts, so you can make the right changes faster - and not waste money and time, lose market share, and work harder and harder to earn less and less.

If you want something different... you have to DO something different.

This book is about the 'something different'.

It's about what you can do now to adapt and grow. Ultimately, it's about how to get everything you need from your business, so you can have everything you want in your life.

Your first step to benefit is to toss the Kryptonite mindset aside. Just flush it.

As you read on, keep this in mind...

WHAT MAKES PERSUASIVE SALES COPY - PERSUASIVE

The REAL masters of the business universe know what needs to be done and call in the best experts to do what it takes to get the job done right the first time.

Money buys knowledge, talent, experience, accuracy and speed!

Ignore the siren call.

Open your mind and know...

The answers to the most important questions about how to transform your business into the steady-growth, high-profit enterprise you want it to be, are right here for you. The information in this book is SOLID GOLD. It works.

Now – give me a big smile... and go to the page.

WHAT MAKES PERSUASIVE SALES COPY – PERSUASIVE... COVETED SECRETS REVEALED!

Rogue Copywriting Genius Breaks The Silence To Reveal Persuasion Secrets Powerful Enough To Hold Your Best Prospects Spellbound & Double - Triple Or Maybe Even Quadruple Your Sales...

by Master Copywriter & Direct Marketing Expert Russell J. Martino

Revealed in this chapter...

- UNRAVELING THE MYSTERY OF PERSUASIVE COPY: 3 things you MUST KNOW to write persuasive copy – or to be able to read copy and know if it is persuasive enough to get attention and sell. Knowing this gives you a HUGE advantage!
- BLINDING FLASHES OF BRILLIANT INSIGHT that will punch up the persuasive power of your copy and virtually guarantee they read every word.

WHAT MAKES PERSUASIVE SALES COPY - PERSUASIVE

- THE STRUCTURE OF PERSUASION – an explanation of the major ideas and specific elements that make a sales message persuasive and make a sales letter complete. Without this, your chances of selling very much at all...are dead on zero!

Dear friend and fellow business owner,

When Jim contacted me to help market his industrial lighting systems, he had earned three fortunes in three different businesses. By any standard, he was a successful entrepreneur with the well-honed ability to start a business from scratch, build a successful company. And make a fortune.

But as successful as he was in deal-making and face-to-face selling, with no direct marketing experience and no experience in direct response copywriting - he hadn't cracked the code on how to get in the door and sell $100,000+ advanced lighting systems to new car dealerships.

His team of salespeople did well selling to manufacturers with huge facilities.

But after a year of phone work and sales people knock doors, only one lighting system had been sold to a new-car dealership - and that dealership was owned by a friend.

Full disclosure...

I had never sold $100,000+ lighting systems. *I was only vaguely aware they existed.* And other than buying cars, I had never done business with new car dealerships.

However I have extensive expertise in sales and direct marketing - and a boiling passion for writing direct response copy that can get past any gatekeeper – grab any good prospects attention – and sell any product or service at any price point – the more expensive the better.

Given that experience, it was no surprise as Jim told his story... the solution became clear.

His single automobile-dealership-client agreed to appear in a 17-minute video I produced. And we sent that video, with a two-page letter, by Fed Ex to 68 car dealerships in the Houston area.

The letter convinced people to watch the video.

The video sold them on the lighting system.

Results came fast. The first call came in three days. And the sale was made.

Over the next seven months, the video and the letter, with good telephone follow-up, resulted in over one million dollars in sales. *Cash in the bank.* And that put the company on the map.

NO SALES FOR A YEAR -VS- $1 MILLION+ IN SALES IN 7-MONTHS... WHAT MADE THE DIFFERENCE?

The only difference between a year with NO SALES - and HAULING IN OVER ONE MILLION DOLLARS IN SALES in seven-months – was the right direct marketing campaign, which took the form of a well-planned, seventeen-minute video and a two-page sales letter sent to a handful of good prospects.

Imagine sending a video and a sales letter to a group of good prospects – and hauling over a million dollar in sales for the effort.

WHY IT WORKED – PART 1

I'd like to say it worked because I'm an insanely brilliant marketing genius who writes copy so persuasive, people read it, drop what they're doing and rush to buy my clients product.

And while there may be some truth to that ... that is most decidedly NOT why a two page letter and seventeen minute video pulled over a million dollars in sales.

First and foremost...

WHAT MAKES PERSUASIVE SALES COPY - PERSUASIVE

It worked because Jim wanted to crack the automobile market wide open. He had a vision. He wanted to be THE dominant force selling new-technology lighting systems to new car dealers.

More importantly –

Jim is a winner – committed to winning.

Even though he had spent a bundle *'trying'* to get a foot-hold in the market - and nothing had worked - he was not discouraged. He didn't tuck his tail between his legs and slink away.

He believed in his product.

He knew that with the right approach, he would dominate the market.

And he knew the financial rewards for doing that were OFF THE CHART HIGH. *So high that investing more than expected to make it happen... just didn't matter.*

And MUCH to his credit...

Jim was willing to act!

He wanted to sell new-technology lighting systems to new car dealers. He couldn't figure out how. So he sought out someone with the know-how and experience to solve the problem.

And again, much to his credit, when Jim heard my fee for designing the sales campaign and writing the copy he believed would get him what he wanted - he didn't whine, cry or try to play some silly negotiating game to get a lower price.

Instead, he correctly reasoned that, *like his lighting systems that give car dealership owners a HUGE payback in electricity savings starting the first month...* the right direct marketing campaign would crack the market wide open – and that would be worth millions.

In other words, Jim's primary driver in working with me was VALUE – not price.

Up to this point, Jim had done what many business owners do to *try* and increase sales. He threw money at the problem. He tried one tactical action after another. And hoped for the best.

The problem with tactical marketing is;

> "Tactics without strategy is the noise before defeat."
> Sun Tzu – *The Art of War*

Throwing money at a marketing problem and hoping for the best is a bad idea. It almost never works. And when it does, its blind luck – you cannot repeat.

- Image-marketing, branding, social media, and so-called Internet marketing, *(whatever that means),* had all failed. *Jim called it "a complete waste of time."*
- Expensive ads that ran repeatedly in the trade-journals pulled zero response.
- Beautiful color brochures by an award-winning graphics designer made no difference.
- Technical papers that 'prove' the systems save a fortune in electricity didn't help.
- The impressive Web site loaded with dazzling photos, technical specifications, contact information and more – seemed to make no difference.
- He couldn't get past the gatekeepers. He couldn't get his prospects attention. Sales people couldn't reach decision-makers. No one returned calls. Nothing worked.

Tactics without strategy really is the noise before defeat.

Each of these things failed for the same reason.

They were one-off tactical actions that presented mountains of company-centric and product-centric information no one cares about. *(Buy from me because I have a slick brochure!)*

WHAT MAKES PERSUASIVE SALES COPY – PERSUASIVE

The slick brochures and impressive engineering diagrams were pretty. But unless you're selling dresses for a garden party, people don't care about pretty.

Created with no understanding of what it takes to get attention in a crowded marketplace where no one wants to be bothered, *and 100 people a day are clamoring for just five-minutes of your time,* those tactical 'stabs in the dark' at the market failed.

This is the same challenge you face.

Regardless of what you sell, from lighting systems to expensive professional services...

...If you can't *get and hold* your prospects attention in a crowded marketplace - *and get them thrilled about doing business with you...* you never do half as well as you could.

Jim had spent a bundle trying to sell lighting systems. Everything that was *supposed to work,* including sending salespeople to dealerships and knocking doors, didn't.

And that's when a mutual friend, the president of our bank, referred Jim to me.

WHY IT WORKED – PART 2

So when all else failed, why did a straight-forward direct response marketing and copywriting campaign work to the tune of a million dollars in sales over a few months?

It worked because I developed the RIGHT MESSAGE. And because...

WE GOT THE RIGHT MESSAGE TO THE RIGHT MARKET.

The difference between the right message *and any other message...* is the difference between being seen as a problem solver *your prospect wants to speak with...* verses being seen as just another chump waving hands and yelling 'buy from me'- *your prospect can't wait to get rid of.*

Experience this truth for yourself...

Think about what gets your attention and moves you to action - *verses* - what you glance at as you toss junk mail in the trash, change the channel or click away from a Web site.

Next...

Think about messages you find interesting enough to look over before you toss them aside - *verses* - a message so compelling you turn up the volume, join the list, read the letter, watch the video, fill out the form, request the report, make the call, or simply buy the product.

Why do you dismiss one message with a quick glance? While another message gets your attention. Holds your interest. And persuades you to act?

WHY YOU BUY...

How can one marketing message be of no interest, while a different message about the same product can be made so interesting, you read every word and take the requested action?

The real question is, "What motivates you?" What gets and holds YOUR attention? What makes a product or service so irresistible you want it and you want it now?

Psychologists tell us...

If you WANT something you don't have, *like a new car, a better job, or enough money to retire in style ten years ahead of schedule, travel the world and still be rich forever...*

Or if you HAVE something you don't want, *like crooked teeth, excess body fat, the heart-break of psoriasis, or a business that does a tiny fraction of what it could...* it creates stress.

Psychologists call the stress of WANTING SOMETHING YOU DON'T HAVE, or HAVING SOMETHING YOU DON'T WANT cognitive dissonance.

WHAT MAKES PERSUASIVE SALES COPY – PERSUASIVE

According to the experts...

The desire to relieve cognitive dissonance and eliminate the stress of having something you don't want or wanting something you don't have, drives buying behavior more than any other factor.

No one buys because some chump shows up in real life or online waving hands and barking about how great their product is.

You buy because you have an itch you want to scratch; a need, wish, want or desire you want to satisfy, something you want to HAVE, BE or DO.

You buy because you are unhappy, uncomfortable or upset about something – and want to fix it.

You buy because you have something you want to keep, protect and not lose.

You buy because you want to accomplish, have or achieve something – and you are willing to spend money on a product or service if you believe it will help you get what you want.

Ultimately, you buy because you want to MAKE something happen - STOP something from happening. Or BE PREPARED in case it does happen.

> To get attention and build the kind of desire it takes for your prospect to WANT what you sell - and want it from YOU - it's critical you know what your prospects really want, which is NEVER a product or service.

And it's critical you do a great job demonstrating how your product will satisfy their desire. Scratch their itch. And give them what they want.

The decision to buy...

Emotion drives the decision to buy.

You don't buy a product because it's there. You buy a product or service because you believe having it will help you get something you want – or avoid something you don't want.

You don't want a new car because of anti-lock brakes or rack and pinion steering.

You want a new car because ... you work hard and deserve to travel in style. And besides, *unlike so many others*, you can afford a nice new car. So why deprive yourself.

What does that have to do with anti-lock brakes?

Buying is an emotional decision. That's why it takes engaging, emotion-driven copy to get attention, hold interest, and get someone excited about doing business with you.

To craft strong emotion-driven messages you have to know what your prospects REALLY WANT, which is never a product or service.

You need to understand the PAIN your prospects experience by not having what they want. And you have to understand the JOY getting what they want will bring them.

We want the THRILL of victory. And want to avoid the AGONY of defeat. Fear of loss and desire for gain are what drive people to act. Fear of loss is more powerful.

> Engaging emotion like a harpist engages strings on the harp – while keeping your message focused on what your prospects really want - is what makes persuasive copy persuasive.

With emotion...

You have the image of a self-made man *(success)* with rugged good looks *(desirable – what every woman wants)* cruising the open road

WHAT MAKES PERSUASIVE SALES COPY - PERSUASIVE

(independence – freedom) – in a powerful new automobile *(strength – power – money - no limits)...*

*...*With a beautiful woman by his side *(satisfaction – happiness – desire fulfilled).*

Without emotion...

All you have a commercial all about front disk brakes.

Which would you prefer?

Back to Jim and why a simple direct marketing campaign that sold over a million dollars in new-technology lighting systems over seven-months worked.

The video and two page sales letter worked because...

I determined what business owners who are good prospects for $100k-plus new-technology lighting system really want.

And we got the RIGHT MESSAGE to the RIGHT MARKET.

> **INSIDER TIP**: The right message *scribbled on scratch paper in crayon* – delivered to the right prospect – will outsell fancy brochures designed by award-winning graphic artists – every time.

To create that message I applied the straight-forward principles of *salesmanship in print.*

The principles were handed down by the real copywriting geniuses all serious copywriters today owe a debt of gratitude to - men like John E. Kennedy, Claude Hopkins, Robert Collier, John Caples and Eugene Schwartz to name a few.

Anyone can learn these principles.

But learning them will not make you a great copywriter any more than learning music theory will make you a great composer.

25

However, knowing what makes persuasive copy persuasive empowers you to read copy and objectively know if the message is persuasive. Or if it's just a word salad served on paper.

Now with that said...

Let's examine what makes persuasive copy persuasive.

THREE THINGS YOU MUST KNOW TO WRITE PERSUASIVE COPY...

Before Jim started his new-technology lighting company he had made millions developing commercial property and selling in person, face-to-face, one-to-one.

But selling in print, video or any media is different than selling face to face.

Instead of telling the same story a hundred times to a hundred people – you tell the very BEST story you can tell one time. *That way... an unlimited number of prospects can get your best presentation entirely at their convenience, with no inconvenience to you. And no need for appointments, discussion, or any conversation at all.*

This is ONE to MANY selling.

To be effective, your one-to-many message must;

1) get attention; 2) hold attention, and; 3) be compelling enough to get your prospect to realize they'd have to be crazy to not do business with you.

Getting this kind of response from a one-to-many presentation in any form, sales letter, video, special report, audio, sales funnel copy, email, or anything else... never happens by accident.

Sales copywriting – that is, writing copy for the express purpose of getting someone to stop what they're doing, consume your message, and give you money - is more like SELLING and less like WRITING. But

WHAT MAKES PERSUASIVE SALES COPY - PERSUASIVE

you are writing. And that makes copywriting SALESMANSHIP IN PRINT.

How do you do that?

How do you write engaging messages rivet attention and get your prospects so excited they CAN'T WAIT to do business with you, to the exclusion of all other?

How do you write persuasive copy that SELLS?

There are thousands of books on consumer behavior, persuasion, influence and sales. And many more on how to write response-pulling copy.

So if you want to write response-pulling copy for yourself - or be able to recognize it when you see it *and know why it's persuasive* - so you can choose a good copywriter...

...You can read few thousand books to learn the secrets of how to sell in print.

Or you can apply these insider secrets - and your ability to write persuasive copy will improve. While your ability to spot good copy – *and know why it's good* - will soar.

WHAT PEOPLE WANT & WHY THEY BUY 3 INSIDER SECRETS

SECRET #1

No one wants products or services, especially you or the people you sell to.

We want solutions, outcomes and experiences. You want your problems solved. You want your sales to soar. You want your bank account to grow. You want to be healthy, happy and rich.

Your prospects are just like you. So if your message drones on forever about how great your product is, which is what most sales copy does, your copy is doomed right from the start.

Why is product-centric and company-centric copy doomed from the very start?

Because no one cares about your product or service - *not even people who give you their hard earned money to buy it.*

Your prospects are like you. They care about what they want to have, be and do. They care about what they want to achieve or avoid.

They care about what scares them. And they care about what excites them.

The key to hold attention and sell is to *focus on what your prospects want*. Which are solutions, outcomes and feelings... not products or services.

Products and services are vehicles that deliver solutions and outcomes. They are what solves the problem, makes fear go away or opens the door to health, happiness and wealth.

Position your product or service as THE SOLUTION that will give your prospects what they want most in their business or their life... and your sales message is irresistible.

Make your message about ANYTHING ELSE - and your prospect will dismiss you with the same speed you dismiss anything you're not interested in.

SECRET #2

People buy for THEIR reasons not yours.

Your prospects couldn't care less about how fancy your widget is or why you want them to buy.

They don't care that you've been in business for 25 years. They don't care that you've won awards. They don't care that 'you care'.

WHAT MAKES PERSUASIVE SALES COPY - PERSUASIVE

Like you, your prospects care about what's on their mind.

They care about solving their problems.

They care about their family. They care about their future.

They care about getting what they want. Avoiding what they don't want. And they care about being happy, healthy, attractive, loved, respected and rich.

If you want to influence someone, talk about - what's on THEIR mind. Talk about what's in it for THEM. Not about what's interesting to you.

Make your message about your prospect, and they pay attention. Make it about anything else and your message is an interruption. And people hate being interrupted!

Your prospects' motivations are all that matters. *And that means...*

To write compelling copy...

- You have to know what your prospects want - and make that the centerpiece of your message.

- You have to demonstrate how your product will *give them what they want* – which is to solve a problem, satisfy a desire or make their life better in some real way.

- You have to disqualify alternatives.

- You have to provide credible proof YOUR solution is the best solution for them. And YOU are the best person/company to provide that solution.

- You have to give them strong reasons to buy and strong reasons to buy FROM YOU.

- You have to make an offer so good your prospect finds it irresistible. *If you've done all the above well... your prospect wants your product long before you present the offer.*

- You have to create a *sense of urgency* so strong – NOTHING will stop your prospect from making the purchase. Right now. This moment.

SECRET #3

It's all about the customer and NEVER about you, the company, the product, the service or anything not important to your prospect.

YOU are your favorite subject on earth. You think about your problems, your plans, your health, your family, your business, your finances, your hopes and dreams and your leisure time.

You and people you love and care about – or problems or situations you have to deal with - are on your mind about 100% of the time.

Your prospects are the same.

Everything in your sales message not DIRECTLY related to your customer is OFF TOPIC. An invitation for them to get bored and be gone. *Just like that.*

Make your copy about your prospect and they pay attention.

Make your copy about anything else, *like how great your product is, how long you've been in business or how much you 'care'* - and your sales message is tossed away with the same instant disregard you toss junk mail in the trash can.

So how do you talk about your product - if no one cares?

Good question! I'm glad you asked.

The secret is to tie everything to your prospect.

If you sell a six-thousand dollar program to restore function to damaged nerves in the arms or legs, you could write a letter that says...

> Hi, I'm Doctor John Doe. I've been helping people with nerve damage for twenty years. I've written books, won awards and speak at conferences. I'm an expert. Our

WHAT MAKES PERSUASIVE SALES COPY - PERSUASIVE

office is great. Our people are great. Our treatment is great. Our equipment is state of the art. If you have nerve damage, we can help. We love our patients. We love referrals. *We care!*

OR - YOU COULD START OUT SOMETHING LIKE THIS...

A PERSONAL MESSAGE from Dr. John Doe on something that may affect your HEALTH, HAPPINESS, MOBILITY & QUALITY OF LIFE – plus some good news about Audrey!

"Living on Borrowed Time"

Don't let this happen to you!

The first symptoms may be only a mild tingling or numbness or a slight loss of feeling in your arms, legs or feet.

As damage grows and you begin to lose feeling in your feet, it's easy to lose your balance. Easy to fall. Easy to hurt yourself.

With time, or practically overnight, that 'mild tingling' in your hands or feet can turn into screaming pain – the kind you can't ignore – the kind that lays you low and destroys your quality of life.

Eventually peripheral nerve damage can get so bad it lands you in a wheel chair.

If you feel tingling in your arms or legs, if your hands or feet feel numb but don't hurt – this is especially dangerous. Because without pain to tell you something is wrong ... you may not realize you're dealing with a problem that can explode into life-altering pain and destroy your quality of life.

> If you feel tingling or numbness in your feet or legs ... if you've lost feeling and can't feel your feet ... if you're worried about losing your balance, falling or dropping things - even without pain...
>
> YOU ARE SUFFERING FROM NERVE DAMAGE - AND THAT MEANS YOUR HEALTH - MOBILITY & YOUR QUALITY OF LIFE
>
> MAY BE AT SERIOUS RISK...
>
> If you experience these symptoms... this is the most important thing you will ever read - because this explains what's happening to your nerves. Why you're at risk. And more importantly...
>
> How To Get Out Of Harm's Way
>
> Reading this could save from a world of grief. So for your own good...
>
> Please Read Every Word
>
> Dear Friend,

FYI – this copy has produced over $200k *per month* for 18-months and counting as of the date of this publication.

Another example of how to make your message all about your prospect.

Like the above letter, this is a big success.

> If you have any assets at all...Stocks, bonds, IRAs, 401ks, royalties, rental property... anything of value, including a boat, RV, airplane, expensive jewelry, a collection of coins, stamps, guns, art, musical instruments or ANYTHING valuable you want to keep... and don't want confiscated by the government or taken from you by

WHAT MAKES PERSUASIVE SALES COPY - PERSUASIVE

con-men, lawyers, or anyone... This may be the most important letter you've ever read.

Lee Bellinger's Personal System to Short-Circuit Con-Men, Crooked Lawyers, the IRS & Government Bureaucrats – What They Don't Want You to Know...

JUST IN: How to Take Control of Your Legal Needs & Protect Yourself As the "You-Know-What" Hits the Fan...

NO Changes to Fix Legal System Coming From Congress! As Frivolous Law Suits Heat Up & Obama Debt Bombs Go Off Everywhere This Is Your BLACK BOOK OF INSIDER SECRETS – Your ULTIMATE GUIDE to Get Ready Without Legal Fees - Get the Target Off Your Back & Protect Your Assets From Frivolous Lawsuits - Greedy Trial Lawyers & Bloodsucking Bureaucrats - Who Want YOUR Money...

Revealed in this letter;

Why the odds of YOU being charged with a crime by the government or sued for everything you own in a civil action and sucked into a terrible money-sucking legal battle you MUST fight or risk losing everything... are higher now than at any time in American history... and what to do about it.

Why not taking proper steps to protect your privacy and secure your assets from government seizure, civil suit, crooked lawyer tricks and over-reaching bureaucrats could eventually wreck your health and send you to the poor house. Without proper steps you are not safe. No one is immune!

Why 'good intentions' don't help and often hurt in legal matters. Plus proprietary insider-secrets and street-smart steps to secure your privacy, make your assets INVISIBLE and UNTOUCHABLE to anyone who would do you harm. And take control of your legal needs in a world gone mad!

Dear Valued Friend,

It gives me no joy to bring you this news. But I must.

You deserve to know the facts.

ONE MORE EXAMPLE...

If division of assets, child custody, child support, paying or receiving alimony... AND YOU NOT BEING TAKEN ADVANTAGE OF IN A DIVORCE matters to you at all... this will be the most important thing you ever read.

Navigating Divorce

From Chaos To Clarity...

What you must KNOW to protect your interests and not be

ripped off or taken advantage of in a negotiation, mediation

or in open court, in a high-asset divorce proceeding.

In this briefing...

Shattered dreams – Why divorce may be the most stressful time of your life... and what you must do to avoid mistakes that may scar you emotionally, destroy you financially and cause you years of regret.

What's REALLY at stake – and what you MUST KNOW about the legal system to protect your rights, get a fair settlement... and never be taken advantage of in any

WHAT MAKES PERSUASIVE SALES COPY – PERSUASIVE

way, by anybody, especially opposing counsel.

CONTESTED or UNCONTESTED – What it means to win. PLUS – How to avoid a long, expensive fight over assets, custody or anything - and still get what you want. And what to do if that doesn't workout.

Dear Friend,

This is important, so let's get straight to it.

Divorce is painful.

ANOTHER EXAMPLE...

EXTREMELY LIMITED: Fewer than one in every one thousand investors reading this can be approved for $6,519 in free wealth-building tools. Acceptance is on a first-come, first-serve basis. Please read this letter carefully and reply accordingly. — Michele Ress, CFO, The MoneyShow

To thank you for the friendship and loyalty

you have shown to all of us here at The MoneyShow...

Kim Githler, Chair and CEO of MoneyShow

I want you to have the most valuable gift we have ever offered anybody:

Subscriptions to top investment advisories and investment tools others pay $6,519 for — yours, FREE!

Dear Friend and Fellow Investor,

You know what you're doing. You're successful. You've built a great portfolio.

Congratulations — now, it's time to take your investment profits to the next level!

I'm Kim Githler. As the Chair and CEO of The

MoneyShow — the world's largest financial conference company — I host tens of thousands of serious investors each year at our conferences in Orlando, Las Vegas and other cities, as well as our online exhibitions and webinars.

Like you, I'm also an investor. I watch the market like a hawk. Manage my own investments. And I do well: I started with almost nothing and built an impressive portfolio.

I've done so well because I have a huge advantage over most investors — an advantage I can now share with you.

The thing is, when it comes to investing, I'm probably the luckiest person you've ever met — and for one, simple reason...

I work with many of the most successful investment experts in Wall Street!

In the 32 years that I've owned and managed MoneyShow, I've worked with many superstars of the investment world.

From market wizards and option gurus, to forex, commodities, and forecasting experts, these superstars include many of the smartest, most highly regarded people in Wall Street.

Louis Navellier, John Bollinger, Larry McMillan, Jim Stack, Linda Raschke, Roger Conrad, Gary Shilling; to name a few; I've known them all for decades.

We love talking shop. We compare notes, discuss strategy, share tips and ideas. We act on the strategies and information that we learn from each other — and the profits are often substantial.

WHAT MAKES PERSUASIVE SALES COPY – PERSUASIVE

Now, these wealth-building experts

can give you the same advantage

that has helped me do so well

The truth is, my entire life has been dedicated to giving you the same advantages I enjoy: To learn from Wall Street professionals who manage billions and build fortunes so you can…

Earn impressive profits by harnessing the power of their time-tested wealth-building strategies…

Lock in solid, double-digit yields with these experts' income-multiplying tactics, and…

Protect your principal and profits and secure your future.

…Because mastering the art of protecting capital and building wealth gives you the kind of freedom and security most people can only dream of.

This is straight from

the heart…

I want you to have it all — every strategy, every investment recommendation, and every market commentary these leading experts release…

ANOTHER EXAMPLE...

Imagine identifying HUNDREDS of stocks that deliver 184.2% to 550% returns IN LESS THAN ONE YEAR. With a way to identify STRONG STOCKS positioned to deliver that kind of growth... you have EVERYTHING you need DOUBLE... TRIPLE... even QUADRUPLE your wealth year after year. And now... for a limited time... and a measly $9 bucks... you can!

Introducing

Push Button Profits

THE ONLY ADVANTAGE YOU NEED to PICK STOCKS that can DOUBLE ... TRIPLE & QUADRUPLE YOUR WEALTH IN A SINGLE YEAR OR LESS... all with a click of the mouse. PUSH BUTTON PROFITS ARE REAL!

This changes everything!

In this briefing:

The FASTEST WAY to spot big winners — I'm talking TOP rated stocks vetted by a team of experts and positioned to DOUBLE, TRIPLE even QUADRUPLE in value... and skyrocket your wealth in 2016.

How PUSH BUTTON PROFITS makes picking big winners FASTER, EASIER & SAFER than ever... now spotting stocks ready to deliver FAST double-digit gains that can pad retirement is easy. Now you can build a financial safety-net that gives you peace-of-mind. Now you can!

The only strategy you need to help you PROTECT YOUR WEALTH in 2016, identify hundreds of TOP RATED stocks ready to explode in growth ... and build the kind of portfolio that makes investing fun... and life a pure joy!

Dear Investor,

With over 12,000 stocks to choose from, staying safe and picking winners is a challenge.

Spend just 1 minute evaluating each stock, and it will take you over 200 hours non-stop hours to review them all.

There are too many stocks and too much data that

WHAT MAKES PERSUASIVE SALES COPY – PERSUASIVE

must be considered for an individual to even try to ...

1) Review 12,000 stocks and weed out the risky ones;

2) Zero in on strongest stocks that make the most sense to invest in and hold in your portfolio, and;

3) Identify the BEST of the strong stocks with the highest probability of holding value and giving you fast, potentially explosive growth.

Without this kind of rigorous analysis your choices are limited and your risks are higher. Investing without DEEP market intelligence is like playing dice with your hard-earned cash.

Because for every stock you consider, there may be a dozen more with stronger financials, bigger markets and a higher probability of explosive growth.

Most investors never solve this problem.

Maybe that's why a UC Davis and UC Berkeley research study shows that only about 1% of all investors ever beat the market average.

The good news is there is a solution.

ANOTHER EXAMPLE...

If you've been injured in an auto accident, this may be the most important message you ever read. For your own good... please read every word.

Don't Be Cheated!

Don't Risk Being Tricked - Cheated or Conned Out Of The Full Legal Compensation You Deserve For Your Injury!

A FREE SERVICE FOR ACCIDENT VICTIMS

> xxx-xxx-xxxx
>
> URGENT MESSAGE FOR ACCIDENT VICTIMS
>
> It's one of the oldest tricks in the book. And if you fall for it, you can kiss thousands or maybe even tens of thousands of dollars that may be rightfully yours goodbye.
>
> Negotiating directly with an accident victim who doesn't understand their rights and has no idea how much compensation they are rightfully due ... is how insurance companies trick people into signing away their rights and accepting a tiny fraction of the compensation rightfully due.
>
> Don't let this happen to you...

BLINDING FLASHES OF INSIGHT FROM COPYWRITING GENIUSES THE BEST OF THE BEST TODAY – LEARNED FROM...

JOHN E. KENNEDY, the marketing and copywriting genius who laid the foundation all great copywriters stand on today taught MANY things. Including...

1. When we multiply nothing by ten thousand we still have nothing as a result.
2. When we multiply a pretty picture, a catch-phrase, or the mere name of a firm or an article a thousand times, we have comparatively nothing as a result.
3. But when we multiply one thousand times a good, strong, clearly expressed Reason Why a person should buy the article we want to sell, we then have impressed, through advertising, one thousand

WHAT MAKES PERSUASIVE SALES COPY – PERSUASIVE

more people with that reason than if it had been told verbally to one person by the same salesman.

4. "ADVERTISING is Salesmanship-on-paper. It is a means of multiplying the work of the salesman, who writes it, several thousand-fold."

5. The difference in RESULTS between copy written by two equally bright men (or women) may be, and often is, 80%, though the same space be used in each case to sell the same article.

6. That difference consists, first of all, in the quality of argument, the "Reason Why' that each of the two lines of copy contains - and next in the Personality with which these arguments have been invested in either copy, so as to strike the most Responsive Chord with the class of readers aimed at.

7. "True advertising is just Salesmanship multiplied."

ROBERT COLLIER, one of the greatest copywriters on any short list, taught;

1. To connect with a prospect – you must 'enter a conversation already going on in the readers mind.'

2. Six prime motives lurk beneath all purchase decisions; love, gain, duty, pride, self-indulgence, and self-preservation.

3. Two primary reasons a person will buy; 1) he believes he will get something from his decision, and; 2) he believes he may lose something if he doesn't buy. And fear of loss is a more powerful motivator than desire for gain.

CLAUDE C. HOPKINS, one of the greatest copywriter to ever live taught;

1. Advertising is multiplied salesmanship.

2. Its principles are the principles of salesmanship. Successes and failures in both lines are due to like causes. Thus every

advertising question should be answered by the salesman's standards.

3. The only purpose of advertising is to make sales; not for general effect; not to keep your name before the people. And not to aid your other salesmen.
4. The more you tell the more you sell.
5. Bring all your good arguments to bear. Cover every phase of your subject. One fact appeals to some, one to another.
6. Platitudes and generalities roll off the human understanding like water from a duck. They leave no impression whatever.
7. The weight of an argument may often be multiplied by making it specific.

Another great on anyone's short list, **JOHN CAPLES**, may have been the first to explain that people buy for emotional reasons, not practical ones. Approximately one-third of his sales message focused exclusively on how the prospect would 'feel' with the product.

Caples saw the product strictly as a means to an end.

> The product or service is the vehicle that delivers the emotional benefits your prospects so desperately want... feelings of security, satisfaction, respect, love, adventure, power, success and so on.

Caples taught MANY things. Including;

1. Capture the prospects attention. Nothing happens unless something in your ad, mailing or commercial makes the prospect stop long enough to pay attention to what you say next. *(by focusing on what the prospect really wants)*

WHAT MAKES PERSUASIVE SALES COPY - PERSUASIVE

2. Maintain the prospect's interest. Keep the ad, mailing or commercial focused on the prospect, on what he or she will get out of using your product or service. *(Remember – people buy for THEIR reasons, not yours.)*
3. Move the prospect to favorable action. Unless enough "prospects" are transformed into "customers", your ad has failed, no matter how creative.
4. *(Moving a prospect to action requires a big idea to get their attention, a strong emotional appeal to hold their interest, a rock-solid sales argument that makes perfect sense, and an irresistible offer, with an iron-clad guarantee.)*

PUT ALL THIS TOGETHER...

And you start to have a good idea of the kind of thinking that goes into writing sales copy strong enough to get attention. Hold interest. And compel action.

But how do you do it? Where do you start? How do you begin?

Writing winners is no easy task.

Persuasive copywriting – the kind that gets attention, holds interest and compels a good prospect to buy your product or service - never happens by accident.

It takes knowledge, conviction, research, thought, organization, skill and work to write the kind of letter that can launch a product, turn a company around - or create a flood of inquiries and sales.

WITH THAT SAID, LET'S EXAMINE...

1. QUESTIONS that must be answered to write a persuasive sales letter
2. The INVISIBLE STRUCTURE of a persuasive sales letter;
3. STEPS it takes to write a persuasive ONE TO MANY sales letter.

ANSWER THESE QUESTIONS AND YOU ARE ON YOUR WAY TO WRITING A WINNING PROMOTION.

1. What's the goal of your promotion? New leads? Sell to first-time buyers. Sell to existing customers? Get a YES from prospects who have not bought yet?

2. Who is your IDEAL prospect? Describe them in detail; age, race, sex, education, income, experience, beliefs, etc. What makes them ideal?

3. What problem does your product or service solve? Is this a REAL problem? Are your prospects worried about this? Does it keep them up at night? Is it a bad enough problem people are willing to spend money to solve it?

4. What are the consequences of having this problem? Age faster? Earn less? Take unnecessary risk? Miss out on the 'good things' of life? No respect. Not taken seriously. Seen as a failure or someone who doesn't matter?

5. Describe the negative consequences this problem creates. Pain? Fear of loss? Terror of the unknown? Disappointment? Disillusionment? Confusion? Lack of self-confidence? Feeling Lost? Anxiety? Stress. Angst. Upset. Anger? Explain in detail how any that apply, or any others not listed, affect your prospect.

6. What PRACTICAL benefits does your product provide? How will life be easier? How will life be better? Why will they be thrilled they have your product?

7. How will having your product help your prospect get something they want or avoid something you don't want? Why is this a superior solution?

8. What EMOTIONAL benefits does your product provide? Will your prospect have more security? Confidence? Respect?

WHAT MAKES PERSUASIVE SALES COPY – PERSUASIVE

Satisfaction? Better health? Will they be more attractive? Admired? Will they have more fun? More freedom? More confidence? Less fear?

9. Why is your solution superior? And why are YOU the superior person or business to provide it? Why specifically? Who says so? What's your proof? Why should anyone believe you? Spell it out. *Without authority, you have nothing!*

10. Before a buyer buys, they must be convinced; the problem is real, needs to be solved, there is a solution that works – and will work for them. They must be convinced they want the solution from YOU - not the competition. And must be convinced the price is fair, the offer is great, they risk nothing and must act now.

WHY DO ALL THAT WORK?

- Why bother to sit down, research, think and work?
- Why bother to imagine the world through your prospects eyes?
- Why bother to imagine how your prospect feels and why they feel that way?
- Why bother to step into their skin and walk a mile in their shoes?
- Why bother to write all these things down?
- Why bother to do all the work just to write a sales message?
- Why go to the trouble of interviewing people who purchased from you - and a few who turned you down - to find out why they did or didn't buy?
- Why go to the trouble of distinguishing yourself from all others?
- Why spend all the time to answer these questions in detail?

I'm glad you asked!

Because now we are crossing a line that begins to separate the pros from the amateurs in the discipline of copywriting.

The fact is...

Anyone can bang out copy about how great they are. Anyone can brag about a company, a product or a service. You don't have to know beans about persuasion to write like that.

Ultimately and with no disrespect intended...

That kind of 'copywriting' is more like carnival barking.

- Because unless you know what motivates your prospect and why...
- Unless you know what your they really want...
- Unless you understand the pain they feel by not having what they want...
- And unless you have a sense of the joy the will feel when they get it...

Without those answers...

...There's nothing to write about except what you think is important.

But your prospects are like you.

They only care about what THEY think is important.

They are interested *their* life, *their* health, *their* family, *their* future and *their* fortune.

Nobody tells them what to do!

They distain unearned authority.

They do things for THEIR reasons not yours.

And they hate wasting time.

And that means...

Your prospects really are like you. They want what they want.

And before they give anyone their hard-earned money... they must be convinced having that product or service will make their life better.

WHAT MAKES PERSUASIVE SALES COPY - PERSUASIVE

If you don't care enough to research, ask questions and figure out what your prospects really want and why, you disrespect them.

And disrespecting someone is a terrible sales strategy.

And besides that...

Without a sense of personal connection, your message is a just a commercial, *(the kind we turn off or fast-forward through),* instead of a conversation with a friend.

Without understanding - there can be no bridge to connect your product to what your prospect wants. And without that bridge, there is no reason to do business with you.

Without understanding, all you can do is drone on about how great your product is. How long you've been in business. And how much you care.

Sound-alike sales messages *that work equally well for any company with the same product or service* are trite. Boring. Have little impact. And are a waste of money and time to produce.

"Great product. Great company. Lots of awards. Great employees. 25-years in business. Great logo. Quality, Service & Dependability – We Care!"

Blah, blah, blah. Blah, blah, blah. Buy from me!

If that's your message - the ONLY distinguishing factor between you and a competitor is PRICE.

And that makes you a commodity.

So unless your goal is to cut profit to the bone and sell at the lowest price possible, take special care to ANSWER THE QUESTIONS LISTED ABOVE IN DETAIL BEFORE YOU WRITE A WORD

IMPORTANT TIP...
Answering the questions in detail does not guarantee success. But one thing is certain. If a copywriter fails to

> *ask questions similar to those detailed above, odds are near 100% your promotion will fail.*

YOUR NEXT STEP IS...

Understanding the INVISIBLE STRUCTURE OF PERSUASION. This takes some of the mystery out of what makes persuasive copy persuasive.

But before we begin...

Can you guess what PRO FOOTBALL and COPYWRITING have in common?

AMATEURS - PROS & BUSINESS OWNERS... SOMETHING TO THINK ABOUT

In 2014 Recruit757.com, a Web site that tracks NFL recruiting statistics, reported there were 70,147 football players spread across 1,281 institutions, conferences and organizations regulated by the National Collegiate Athletic Association (NCAA).

Of those 70,147 college players, the NFL scouted 6500. Of those 6500 college players scouted by the NFL, 350 were invited to tryout - and 256 were drafted by a pro team.

Of those 606 *best-in-the-game* only 300, or 1.6% of over 70,000 college players that year, made the final cut. Got a contract. And had a rookie year on a NFL team.

Three years later, only 150 of those 300 survived and continued to play pro ball.

In other words...

The *'best of the best'* in college are fodder for a wood-chipper in the NFL.

WHAT MAKES PERSUASIVE SALES COPY – PERSUASIVE

COPYWRITING IS NOT PRO FOOTBALL.

But the strength of your sales message – *which is determined more by the skill of your copywriter than any other factor* - plays a huge role in how much you sell. How much you earn. Your financial future. And maybe even your quality of life.

With stakes that high, getting your sales message right...

...So you can attract business and sell more AT WILL - online or offline - in video, print, sales funnels, email or product launches - is serious business.

Serious enough that since your income depends on it... you may want a pro with a long history of success designing and writing winning campaigns to write for you. Why? *Because talent wins championships.*

IT'S SMART TO STUDY COPYWRITING.

It's smart to know what it takes to write copy strong enough to get your prospect excited about doing business with you.

And if you can SELL IN PRINT as well as Payton Manning or Tom Brady can throw a football... its fine to write your own sales copy.

IT'S ALSO FINE TO ASK YOURSELF...

- Is writing the highest and best use of your time in your business?
- Are you the best qualified to write copy that may bring a flood of sales and cash flow - or a disappointing trickle of business – depending on the writer's ability to connect with your prospects and get them excited about doing business with you?

WHATEVER YOUR ANSWER, ONE THING IS CERTAIN...

The time has come to reveal the INVISIBLE STRUCTURE OF PERSUASION that runs through all persuasive copy in whatever form it takes.

WHAT MAKES PERSUASIVE COPY – PERSUASIVE THE INVISIBLE STRUCTURE...

I mentioned earlier we crossed a line that begins to separate pros from amateurs in the discipline of copywriting.

Now let's go deeper and explore territory many copywriters and few business owners even know exists.

The idea is simple. Persuasive copywriting doesn't happen by accident.

You don't *'luck'* your way into writing a promotion that breaks every sales record. And if by some miracle you do, you won't know why it worked. Or how to do it again.

Trying to write persuasive copy without having a structure of persuasion in mind - is like starting a long journey to *somewhere*, with no idea of where you're going or how to get there. It's like trying to build a house without a blueprint.

If you're thinking...

"I got this! He's talking about an outline".

My response is...

"Excellent thinking Grasshopper! An outline is critical. However it has nothing to do with what I am about to reveal." This is so powerful... it can be a game-changer.

ONE MINUTE REALITY CHECK

Stop for a second and think.

WHAT MAKES PERSUASIVE SALES COPY - PERSUASIVE

Besides providing jobs, delivering a good product or service and so on – the purpose of a business is to make the owner rich – or a whole lot richer.

How much did you gross last year? A million? Two million? Five million? Ten?

Of that, how much did you keep?

How much was YOURS to save, spend on whatever you want, plow back into the business to fuel growth, give away or set aside for investing?

Whatever your answer - the difference between you now – and you with a net worth three or four or five or ten times higher, is SALES and PROFIT in your business.

Since the strength of your message is THE #1 KEY to your sales and profit - that means the strength of your message is also THE #1 KEY to your personal income.

- If your sales copy is weak...
- If your Web copy is weak...
- If your videos, funnels and Webinars are weak...
- If you depend on cut-and-paste swipe files you bought cheap just so you'd have copy for your funnels without spending too much…
- If your email sequences are weak...
- If your messages are easy to understand, but not persuasive... you'll make some sales. But only a tiny fraction of what stronger copy can give you.

WEAK COPY POISONS THE WELL.

Weak copy distinguishes you from no one.

Weak copy makes you sound common, ordinary and non-exceptional.

Weak copy makes you sound like anyone on any street corner saying, *"Buy from me – because I want you to buy from me."*

Weak copy drives people away... *who may have done business with you if only your message was stronger and more persuasive.*

Strong copy is a business-building asset that can deliver a huge ROI as fast as you can get that copy in front of qualified prospects.

My friend Jim with his industrial lighting company discussed earlier – banked a 25 to 1 ROI on the cost of my services in seven months of deploying the campaign.

My purpose in pointing this out is NOT to say 'look at me'.

The purpose is to point out that an investment in STRONG COPY – is an investment that can give you a massive return in a short time – regardless of what you sell.

It is impossible to overstate the real-time, money-in-the-bank value of strong copy.

BACK TO BUSINESS...

If you write your own copy, what you are about to discover won't turn you into a Top Gun Copywriter overnight. But it will help you write more persuasively.

Knowing the invisible structure of persuasion will give you a leg up on the world. The principles apply in all human interaction.

Even with just the basics discussed here, you be able to *recognize great sales copy* when you see it – and KNOW WHY its great copy – instead of just knowing it's great.

You'll be able to *spot weak copy* a mile off. And you'll know how to punch up the persuasive power of your own sales copy, Web copy and so on.

WHAT MAKES PERSUASIVE SALES COPY - PERSUASIVE

If the best use of your time is not writing sales copy - and you depend on others to write copy *that will determine your sales, income and peace of mind...*

With the structure I'm about to reveal;

1) You'll be able to judge the persuasive strength of any copy, and;

2) Before you whip out the checkbook and hire a copywriter, you'll be able to interview the writer, read their copy, and to some extent, evaluate their skill.

ONWARD...

The structure of persuasion includes; the big idea, levels of awareness, chain of logic and emotional appeal. There's more to it than this. Much more.

But without this foundation, nothing else matters. So let pull a Julie Andrews – and start from the very beginning.

THE BIG IDEA

Gary Halbert taught...

If a strong central idea drives your sales message, and your prospect buys into that idea, getting him to buy your product will be easy.

Gary called the 'central idea that drives your promotion' THE BIG SELLING IDEA.

With the BIG IDEA, which is an intriguing proposition or promise that captures attention, woven throughout the message - you hold attention and keep things moving.

When you decide on a BIG IDEA, you know exactly what you're going to write about.

Clayton Makepeace teaches that to be effective, your big selling idea must be simple, unexpected, relevant to your prospect, tangible and concrete, provable beyond doubt, loaded with emotional punch, and presented so it feels like a story.

THE BIG IDEA OF THIS CHAPTER IS...

You can know what makes persuasive copy persuasive – and use that knowledge to write persuasive copy. Spot persuasive copy. Find competent writers. And sell more.

That big idea is revealed in the headline and woven throughout the copy.

The more emotional hot-buttons you push, the more impact your BIG IDEA has. Which is why it's critical to know what your prospects want and fear.

Like a movie trailer that gets you excited... your big idea should be so intriguing, your prospects get excited - and WANT to know more.

For that to happen you have to know who your prospects are. Know what they want. Know how their life will be better by having it. And in a logical, lucid and emotional tone, explain how your product helps them get it.

The Prince of Print, Sir Gary Halbert, was right.

If your prospect buys your BIG IDEA, getting them to buy your product is the easy part.

The BIG IDEA can be hinted at or revealed in the headline. And developed immediately in the copy that follows. So in a few sentences, or a few short paragraphs, you set the stage for everything that follows.

IN PROFESSIONAL COPYWRITING JARGON...

The eyebrow, headline, the copy immediately under the headline – together with the first few sentences, paragraphs or pages that explain the big idea, are called THE LEAD.

WHAT MAKES PERSUASIVE SALES COPY – PERSUASIVE

Gary Bencivenga, one of the greatest copywriters on any short list, said...

> "The lead is where you get your prospect to fall in love with your sales letter."

And that means your FIRST SALE... is selling your prospect on reading your letter.

What's Your Big Idea?

What BIG IDEA can you come up with that will grab your prospects' attention and get them excited about reading your letter or watching your video?

To borrow from Clayton Makepeace...

> What big idea can you tie to your product that is simple, unexpected, relevant to your prospect, tangible and concrete, provable beyond doubt, loaded with emotion, and can be presented so it feels like a story?

Finding the right BIG IDEA *with that kind of fire-power* is the most important step in writing persuasive copy.

Why?

Because without a BIG IDEA – nobody notices and nobody cares.

Without a compelling idea to draw your reader into the sales letter, video, report or whatever form your message takes...

All you have is the average kind of *BUY FROM ME* sales message that feels intrusive and no one pays much attention to.

But with the right BIG IDEA, your prospects give you their attention. And you have a chance to move them to action with your words.

LEVELS OF AWARENESS

In his book *Breakthrough Advertising*, legendary copywriter Eugene Schwartz explained how a prospects 'level of awareness' should determine the message.

The concept is simple. The implications are enormous.

Levels of awareness range from MOST AWARE Level 1, where the prospect knows about you and your product, and wants it or is interested – to LEAST AWARE Level 5, where the prospect has little awareness of the problem. Little to no awareness of the solution. And no awareness of you or your product.

A sales message perfect for Most-Aware prospects will fail miserably with Least-Aware prospects. And vice-versa.

Now back to the big idea and the question of how much time a prospect will spend reading your sales letter.

If you deliver the wrong BIG IDEA for the needs and LEVEL OF AWARENESS of your prospect, your campaign will fall flat regardless of who writes.

FOR EXAMPLE...

If you are an experienced golfer with a good game – a promotion with the BIG IDEA of guaranteeing to shave a few strokes off a beginners' game wouldn't interest you. *And it wouldn't matter who wrote the sales letter.*

Likewise, the BIG IDEA of *Inside Secrets To Turn Pro Fast & Make A Living On The PGA Tour* would be of no interest a new golfer still figuring out which clubs to use.

And it wouldn't matter who wrote the letter.

WHAT MAKES PERSUASIVE SALES COPY - PERSUASIVE

This means you will GET and HOLD attention to the extent your message is on track with your prospects needs and on track with their awareness of the both the problem and possible solutions.

For example, if you cell cybersecurity... your message to someone only vaguely of the problem would be totally different than your sales message to a group of business owners you know have been hacked and had to pay ransom to regain use of their computers.

YOUR FIRST STEPS TO WRITE HIGH-CONVERTING SALES COPY, ARE;

1. Determine WHO you are selling to and determine their level of awareness of the problem and the solution. Do they know the problem exists? Do they know there's a solution? Do they know your product or service can solve the problem?
2. A letter to prospects who know your product solves a problem they have will be dramatically different from a letter to people who don't know they have the problem. Don't know there's a solution. And have never heard of you.
3. Develop a BIG IDEA so intriguing to your prospect – at their level or awareness – they drop what they're doing and give you their full attention.
4. And tipping the hat to great Dan Kennedy...

Developing a BIG IDEA to match your prospects' LEVEL OF AWARENESS is an exercise in MESSAGE TO MARKET MATCH.

Get your message-to-market match right - and with strong copy, a persuasive argument and a great offer and YOU WIN.

Get the message to market match wrong...

And no copywriting magic or top-gun copywriter can save you.

Developing the right BIG IDEA for your prospects LEVEL OF AWARENESS is a non-negotiable requirement of a winning campaign.

SELLING IN PRINT requires more than just the ability to write.

Like an infantry, there are vast legions of writers who can write good, readable copy.

But selling in print requires more than 'readable' copy.

Selling in print require the ability to CONNECT with the reader and deliver a message the reader finds so persuasive, they do what you ask.

In other words, selling in print requires the ability to PERSUADE.

The difference between routine copywriting and sales copywriting is like the difference between a skilled infantry soldier – and an elite Special Forces Warrior with advanced training in strategic awareness, communications, weapons, and tactical mastery,

MOVING ON...

We discussed how pros get attention and get people excited about reading a sales letter by using a BIG IDEA. And we discussed how knowing your prospects LEVEL OF AWARENESS is a key factor in crafting a message that will get and hold their attention.

Next we turn our attention to...

CHAIN OF LOGIC

Emotion drives the decision to buy.

But the decision to keep what you buy - is based on facts and reasons.

Without good reasons and a strong rational to buy - your prospects may want your product and never buy - or buy your product - and return it the next day.

Links in the CHAIN OF LOGIC are the steps you walk your prospect through to help them know 'wanting' your product is fine. But having it is just plain smart!

For example...

WHAT MAKES PERSUASIVE SALES COPY - PERSUASIVE

1. You want your business to grow. You want more sales. More profit. And you want attracting prospects and closing sales to be easier.
2. You know it can be done because you have competitors who are busy all the time and sell more than you every month.
3. You're as smart as them. Probably smarter. If they can do it – so can you.
4. They use direct response copywriting to generate leads. That's how they outsell you every month. You've seen their promotions.
5. You're fed up with working so hard and earning so little. Time is passing. If things don't get better you may have to put off retirement indefinitely.
6. You need a breakthrough. Something that works. You know direct-response sales copy works. But only when you do it right.
7. That's why it's just plain smart to have a proven direct response copywriter plan your proms and write your sales copy. *Or at the very least copy-chief your work.*
8. Direct response copy may be the answer you're looking for – a fast, proven way to generate sales. And a dependable way to build your business and secure the future you want most for yourself and your family.
9. To make sure you have the facts on how to write persuasive copy and how to evaluate a copywriters' ability to sell in print BEFORE you hire them, I prepared a Special Report *The Structure of Persuasion*™ - which you can claim absolutely FREE with your no-risk trial subscription to my monthly newsletter.

And that is a chain of logic that starts with known facts - and leads step-by-step to the reader deciding they'd have to be crazy to not do business with you... or at the very least, contact you to learn more.

With a chain of logic in place – you know where to start your letter, where it's going, and how it's going to get there - before you write the first word.

This is not casual information.

This is part of the invisible structure of persuasion.

And part of what separates direct-response pros with a long list of million-dollar promotions to their credit from all others.

Knowing this does not guarantee big winners. But a sales message without a solid chain of logic the reader can follow, guarantees a tiny response compared what could be.

If you write for yourself...

Apply the chain of logic and your copy can't help but improve.

If you depend on others to write for you, use it to identify writers who can SELL in print.

MOVING ON...

Next we turn our attention to...

EMOTIONAL APPEAL

The decision to buy is based on emotion. And that means, without a strong emotional appeal your copy is flat. Impersonal. And not very persuasive.

You'll recall John Caples taught...

The product or service is the vehicle that delivers the emotional benefits your prospects so desperately want... feelings of security, satisfaction, respect, love, adventure, power, success and so on.

Following in Caples footsteps, copywriting great Clayton Makepeace, one of if not *the* highest paid copywriter alive, is known for being a Dominant Emotion Copywriter.

WHAT MAKES PERSUASIVE SALES COPY - PERSUASIVE

Like Dan Kennedy, Clayton writes laser-focused copy that gets straight to the heart of every emotion, positive and negative, that may impact someone struggling with the kind of problem your product or service can solve.

If you do the research and answer the questions we discussed earlier - before you begin writing – you'll know what your prospects want. You'll know what they worry about. You'll know what keeps them up at night. What they fear, regret and want to avoid.

THE SECRET OF DEVELOPING RICH EMOTIONAL COPY IS...

Think about your prospect. See the world through their eyes. Imagine living their life. Imagine having the problem your product or service will solve.

Imagine how having that problem may affect your prospect. What emotions might they experience? Insecurity? Disappointment? Frustration? Anger? Fear?

Imagine how your product will make their life better.

Will they save time? Save money? Make money. Enjoy better health? Look younger? Feel younger? Be more attractive?

Will it eliminate fear and finally give them what they want?

Make an inventory of all the ways not having the product affects their life... and an inventory of how having the product improves their life.

Then weave that language throughout your copy as you lead your prospect through the chain of logic.

And always remember people do things for their reasons – not yours.

Business owners LOVE copy about their company and their product, *because it's THEIR Company and THEIR product*. But your prospects don't care.

THEY CARE ABOUT WHAT'S IMPORTANT TO THEM.

Saying *Joe The Dentist* has the latest zing-zang FDA approved laser technology that whitens teeth five shades in two hours is interesting – *to Joe the Dentist.*

But because you're a REAL copywriter and you research...

You know how embarrassing it is to have stained teeth. You know the slap in the face self-esteem takes if you keep your lips pressed together or cover your month when you smile – so no one can see those not-so-attractive teeth.

Because you know this...

Instead of writing about Joe the Dentist's zing-zang FDA approved laser, you write about something you KNOW your prospect cares about.

Your message is all about THEM...

> RE: Dazzling white teeth make you even more attractive...
>
> Now You Can Have Dazzling White Teeth & A Smile You Are Proud Of - Life Is Too Short to Wait Another Day...
>
> Dear <first name>,
>
> Do you secretly wish you had cleaner, whiter, brighter teeth?
>
> Do you cover your mouth when you smile because you don't want anyone to see discolored and stained your teeth are?
>
> Do you wish there is a FAST, EASY and AFFORDABLE way for your teeth to be dazzling-white and looking great so you're happy to flash a big smile anytime?

WHAT MAKES PERSUASIVE SALES COPY – PERSUASIVE

Your teeth may be stained for many reasons.

Smoking, regularly drinking coffee, wine or cola - even long-term use of prescription drugs can cause your teeth to look dull and discolored, instead of dazzling and attractive.

It's good to know why your teeth are discolored.

But it's far more important to know that now there is a fast, painless, affordable way for you to have great-looking, dazzling-white teeth... in just a few hours!

When You Are Proud Of Your Teeth & Have The Confidence to Flash A Big Friendly Smile Anytime – Life Just Gets Better!

1. Smiling opens the door to romance! Whether you flash a smile to attract a lover or to excite your romantic partner - nothing is more attractive or exciting than a big smile that says, "I am so glad to see you!" Or "Finally, we're alone!"

2. Your smile is a good indicator of your sense of well-being. Medical research proves the simple act of smiling has an enormous positive impact on a person's health.

3. A confident smile demonstrates self-esteem. A big smile and a confident manner can open more doors and help you get what you want faster than almost anything.

4. A big smile makes you more attractive and makes people more attracted to you. Think about it. When you smile others are more disposed to like you. More eager to do business with you, and happier to help you any way they can.

5. Show up in life with a big smile and people notice. And for a brief moment they forget their troubles. A warm feeling washes over them. And they smile too.

If your teeth embarrass you ... if you hide your smile because you're afraid people may think less of you because your teeth are not in great shape... if you want your teeth to look great so you feel good and are always happy to flash a big smile...

Then call the Joe the Dentist and schedule a FREE EXAMINATION to evaluate your teeth and determine exactly what it'll take to get your teeth dazzling white and looking great.

Life is too short to be embarrassed about anything - especially your teeth.

A simple in-office whitening procedure may be all you need to get your teeth looking great... and you feeling better than ever about them.

This is the perfect opportunity to get those pearly whites... pearly white!

Just pick up the phone and call now - xxx-xxx-xxxx

MOVING ON...

The Structure Of Persuasion™ has many steps. But the purpose here is not to teach every step with all the nuances and turn you into a top-gun sales copywriter.

The purpose is to give you look at what goes into writing persuasive copy. And give you a guide to help spot persuasive copy and evaluate how persuasive a writers copy may be.

WHAT MAKES PERSUASIVE SALES COPY - PERSUASIVE

Big Idea, Levels of Awareness, Chain of Logic and Emotional Appeal are all part of the invisible deep structure of persuasive copywriting.

Knowing these ideas and understanding them well enough to know if they are *present* or *absent* from a piece of sales copy gives you near visionary power to evaluate the persuasive impact of a sales message may have in whatever form it takes.

With these concepts in mind you can read sales copy - know what's missing or what can be done better - and know how to punch up the persuasive impact.

If you want to learn more about the deep structure of persuasive copywriting, email your request to: Russell@StructureOfPersuasion.com

But for now let's move on and discuss specific sections of copy - and what those sections are supposed to achieve.

EVERYTHING IS IMPORTANT.

John Caples taught nothing happens until you capture your prospects attention. And since people buy for emotional reasons... leading with an emotion right from the start will get the attention of anyone with the problem you highlight.

THE EYEBROW

THE EYEBROW:

The eyebrow is first thing on the page, a sentence or two or three above the headline written for the express purpose of letting the reader know who this is for.

If you're sick and tired of being overweight - and ready to lose weight once and for all and keep it off - without crazy diets, excessive exercise or popping pills, this is for you...

> If you're behind on savings and worried you may never have enough money to travel and enjoy the kind of life you want most after retirement, this may be the most important message you ever read.
>
> If you suffer with (INSERT PROBLEM) then this message is for you...

> If you suffer with poor eye sight and are terrified you may lose your sight if something doesn't' change fast, this message from renown eye expert Dr. John Doe is for you...

NEXT...

THE HEADLINE

To quote one of the greatest copywriters in the history or print, my friend and mentor in financial copywriting Clayton Makepeace... *the purpose of the headline is to "grab um by the eyeballs".*

If your headline fails to 'grab um by the eyeballs' and pull the reader into the copy *its game over.* Your letter gets tossed. They click away from your Web page. That's it.

So how do you do it?

How do you write a headline so interesting your prospect notices, so credible your prospect doesn't dismiss it – and so effective your prospect keeps reading?

There are more ways than we have space to discuss.

But here are a few good ones...

WHAT MAKES PERSUASIVE SALES COPY – PERSUASIVE

Tie your headline to breaking news. Ask a burning question. Make a bold statement. Express a common frustration. Create or solve a mystery. Debunk a myth. Attack the enemy. Expose a scandal. Make a startling prediction. Tell a story. And so on.

Take a look at the following examples – and think of how you may adapt these headlines to your product or service.

EUGENE SCHWARTZ
How Modern Chinese Medicine Helps Both Men and Women...

Burn Disease Out of Your Body
Eugene Schwartz
Don't Pay A Penny For This Book Till It DOUBLES Your Power To Learn!

JOHN CAPLES
They Laughed When I Sat Down At the Piano
But When I Started To Play!~

DAVID OGILVY
"At 60 miles an hour the loudest noise in this new Rolls-Royce comes from the electric clock"

GARY HALBERT
The Amazing Diet Secret Of A Desperate Housewife

GARY HALBERT
Wife Of Famous Movie Star Swears Under Oath Her New Perfume Does Not Contain An Illegal Sexual Stimulant!

GARY BENCIVENGA
Trout Spoken Here

GARY BENCIVENGA
Lies, Lies, Lies
We investors are FED UP with everyone lying to us and wasting our money.

WHAT MAKES PERSUASIVE SALES COPY - PERSUASIVE

CLAYTON MAKEPEACE
7 Horsemen of the Coming Stock Market Apocalypse

CLAYTON MAKEPEACE
Forbidden Medicine

The FDA's Secret War Against Your Medical Freedom!

Clayton Makepeace – This launched the then unknown Dr. Julian Witaker HEALTH & HEALING newsletter. Over two years this headline and the letter it introduced resulted in over two million subscribers and about $100 million in sales.

GIVE ME 90 DAYS AND I'LL HELP YOU...

- Avoid headaches, sleep problems, depression and other everyday maladies...
- Unclog heart arteries that cause high blood pressure, stroke and heart attace...
- Tap your body's natural reserves to beat fatigue and have the energy to do the things you love..,
- Avoid – and even reverse – the symptoms of arthritis and most forms of diabetes...
- Disease-proof your body, and add many good years to your life!

DAN KENNEDY

Stop Wasting Money on Advertising Guesswork!

Stop Wasting Time On cold Call Prospecting Grunt Work!

How 'MAGNETIC MARKETING' Will Change Your Business Life Forever – Amazingly Powerful Advertising, Marketing, Direct Marketing, Customer/Client Attraction & Persuasion Strategies REVEALED...

DAN KENNEDY

A very long letter. Required by in-depth discussion of a very serious subject.

You, My Next 'Million Dollar Success Story'?

An invitation limited to 200. An unprecedented opportunity.

A way up and out of the limitations of your business.

A "top secret" Financial Formula and a Moneymaking Plan suitable for just about

ANY business and certainly any true entrepreneur, to be revealed one time only.

WHAT MAKES PERSUASIVE SALES COPY - PERSUASIVE

> **MIKE PALMER** – the most successful financial newsletter promo online EVER.
>
> THE END OF AMERICA
> WARNING: What you are about see is controversial, and may be offensive to some audiences. Viewer discretion is advised.

And in an act of shameless self-promotion...

> **RUSSELL MARTINO**
> If you love olive oil ... if you buy olive oil ... if you cook with olive oil ... if you or
> anyone you care about use olive oil ... please read every word of this eye-opening
> special report ... because what you don't know ... CAN hurt you!
> The Shocking Truth
> About Olive Oil...
> Don't fall for myths, lies and dirty tricks.
> If you want to enjoy the amazing health benefits and the delicious tastes only REAL
> extra virgin olive oil can give you and your family...
> It's critical you read every word!

The secret is to write headlines that are credible, specific and easy to understand. Your headline needs to provoke curiosity, touch a nerve and imply a quick and easy solution.

NEXT...

DECK COPY

Deck copy comes immediately after the headline.

The purpose is to elaborate on the promise or claim made in the headline and bring the reader deeper into the copy.

In my headline, "The Shocking Truth About Olive Oil" – the deck copy, (see above) is:

Don't fall for myths, lies and dirty tricks.

If you want to enjoy the amazing health benefits and the delicious tastes only REAL extra virgin olive oil can give you and your family...

It's critical you read every word!

Don't risk getting ripped off.

HERE'S WHAT YOU NEED TO KNOW.

Next... A quick look at what else goes into writing a persuasive direct response copy.

STEP BY STEP...
FROM BODY COPY – TO CLOSE

1. The body copy, which is the main section of the letter, has a big job.
2. The purpose of the body copy is to;
3. Keep the reader interested – which means the copy needs to be primarily about THEM and not about the company or the product.
4. Build rapport – to do this the copy has to connect on an emotional level. And to connect on an emotional level you have to understand your prospects. You have to see the world through their eyes.

WHAT MAKES PERSUASIVE SALES COPY - PERSUASIVE

5. Establish authority – answer the question, *why should your prospect care at all about who you are or what you have to say? Why should they give you one second of their precious time?*
6. Describe the problem – nothing builds rapport and establishes authority faster than describing the problem better than your prospect can describe it.
7. Describe the pain having the problem causes – describing the pain makes it real. The better you describe the pain – the deeper your rapport will be.
8. Agitate the problem - explain how having the problem makes life miserable on multiple levels and in multiple ways. Open the wound. Make it vivid. Make it real.
9. Introduce spokesperson / establish authority / pour on the proof
10. Story / Solution – I had the same problem. It was terrible. I couldn't sleep. I stayed up nights worrying. Finally, I decided to stop feeling sorry for myself, and figure this out. It was slow going at first. I tried *alternative 1* and failed – *alternative 2* and failed and – *another* that failed. Then finally, in a flash of insight - it hit me. REVEAL THE SOLUTION in strong emotional language that connects with your prospect.
11. Discredit alternatives – get the point across that every other alternative is like a half-built bridge or a ladder missing rungs – or like anything that's average, ordinary and doesn't work all that well.
12. Provide proof your solution is valid – mountains of proof – different kinds of proof – undeniable proof *that handles objections in advance.*
13. Handle Objections In Advance – Strong copy anticipates objections and handles them along the way. Objection handling should be woven throughout the copy – built into the story and specifically addressed in explaining the benefits.

14. Make an irresistible offer – Irresistible means your offer is so good – they simply MUST have it – right now - and are powerless to say no.
15. Detail all the ways life will improve. More money. Better health. More confidence. Respect you deserve. More free time. More productive. More efficient. Safer.
16. Describe all the pain they will avoid - No more sleepless nights. No more worrying about bills. No more saying 'no' to the family when you desperately want to say YES, but can't afford to. No more hiding your mouth when you smile.
17. Introduce price / Reduce price to the ridiculous – Trivialize the purchase price. $300 is less than a dollar a day, less than the cost of a cup of cheap gas-station coffee, less than the price of a candy bar or a package of breath mints. Practically nothing.
18. Sweeten the pot with bonuses – it doesn't matter if you sell Gulfstream jets to billionaires – professional services – or any type of widget under the sun – people LOVE bonuses. HIGH PERCEIVED VALUE but LOW ACTUAL COST bonuses make your offer more irresistible, which means more sales and more profit.
19. Benefit review – Explain all the benefits again – remind your prospect how your widget is going to change everything – whiter whites, brighter brights – no more standing on the sideline wishing you could join the party. Now the world is your playground!
20. Offer review – summarize offer – trivial price again – less than a gallon of gas a day – less than three nights at a cheap motel. $1000 is less than the cost of you and a couple of friends eating out at a decent restaurant once a month. $5000 is less than you'd pay for a cheap used car – practically nothing compared to the benefits of (your widget).

WHAT MAKES PERSUASIVE SALES COPY – PERSUASIVE

21. Reverse the risk with iron-clad guarantee – The stronger and longer the guarantee the fewer the returns. A strong guarantee proves you believe in your product and stand behind what you do, which instills confidence and belief in your prospect.

22. Close the sale – "you stand at a crossroads" – Go one way and the nightmare that is your life will continue – go the other way – and the sun will shine, birds will sing and the good life will finally be yours – no more sleepless nights – no heart-wrenching agony over telling your family no – no more crooked teeth – no more heart break of psoriasis.

23. Here's what to do next – Tell them EXACTLY what you want them to do. Pick up the phone – call us xxx-xxx-xxxx - or – You've seen the facts. You've seen the proof. You know what *(my widget)* can do for you.

24. Now it's up to you. The power to change your life is in your hands. So just click here now – and I'll see you on the other side.

25. Create urgency – Without urgency your prospect will set your sales message aside for now – with the intention of buying from you in a few days or weeks. But that never works out. Bottom line – *you have to create so much urgency – your prospect would rather hack off an arm with a dull knife than NOT buy your widget right now, today.*

26. PS – remind them of a benefit - and how important it is to act now.

> "If you can't describe what you are doing as a process, you don't know what you are doing." - W. Edward Deming
>
> "It is not enough to do your best; you must know what to do, and then do your best." - W. Edward Deming

> "It is not necessary to change. Survival is not mandatory." - W. Edward Deming

THINGS I LEARNED FROM CLAYTON MAKEPEACE 13-REASONS A PROMO CAN FAIL

1. BAD PRODUCT: The product is ill-conceived and people just don't want it.
2. WRONG PRICING: Pricing could be either too LOW or too HIGH. Too low, people may not believe the value is there. Too high, you may price yourself out of the market.
3. WEAK GUARANTEE: A strong guarantee helps close sales. Weak guarantees hurt sales. Typically, the stronger and longer your guarantee, the lower your returns.
4. BAD PREMIUM: Premiums can make a huge difference in response. Premiums add value. Premiums add benefits. Premiums give your prospects more reasons to buy. Strong premiums help close sales. Weak premiums not only do you no good – if the premium is rinky-dink, the prospect may think the main product is rinky-dink too.
5. A BAD LIST: GOOD MESSAGE TO MARKET MATCH = SUCCESS. Deliver the best copy on earth to people with little to no interest in what you sell and the promotion will fail. The stronger your list the more you sell. The stronger your copy the more you sell. But great copy will not convert marginal prospects into responsive buyers. You'll sell more with a list of 10,000 HOT PROSPECTS than with a list of a MILLION who've expressed no interest and may not even have the problem your product or service solves.

WHAT MAKES PERSUASIVE SALES COPY – PERSUASIVE

6. POOR DELIVERY: You can't respond to a promotion you never see. Neither can your prospects. Delivery and open rates on email are so low, smart marketers are returning to DIRECT MAIL with deliver and rates for first class in the high 90%.

7. MAJOR NEWS EVENTS or prospect life events affect readership. People have only so much attention to give to anything. Any BIG news event will use up that attention span – and depress response to almost any kind of sales promotion.

8. THE THEME OF THE MAIN HEADLINE FAILED TO RESONATE. This goes to message to market match. If your headline fails to grab your prospect's attention, nothing else matters, because they'll never see it.

9. THE PROMISED BENEFITS WERE NOT CREDIBLE – Lack of proof. Lack of authority. No testimonials. Unbelievable claims with nothing to back them up.

10. WEAK CLOSE: The closing copy simply didn't convince the prospect to BUY NOW. No urgency. Weak premiums. No compelling reason to act now... before it's too late!

11. COMPLICATED ORDER DEVICE: A complicated order form can stop a would-be buyer in their tracks. Your job is to 'make it easy for your customer to buy' – and the easier you make it – the more you will sell. Simplify the buying process.

12. TECHNICAL PROBLEMS: Severs crash, links that don't work, call centers that don't answer by the third ring ... anything that is not smooth and seamless can hurt response.

13. WRONG MESSAGE – WEAK MESSAGE – CONFUSING, UNBELIEVABLE OR BORING MESSAGE - *OR TO USE SOPHISTICATED INSIDER COPYWRITER TERMINOLOGY –* THE COPY SUCKED

COPY ASSETS THAT SUPPORT DIRECT MARKETING STRATEGIES

- A Master Sales Presentation to engage your prospects. Tell your story. And get them to *WANT* to do business with *YOU*. Your Master Presentation can be in any form, including; a direct-response sales letter, Magalog, Special Report, video, audio and so on.

- Strong Web Copy to engage prospects and lead them through an Invisible Sales Process that results in action. They join your list. Download a special report. Watch your video. Call. Email you. Fill out a form. Set an appointment. Or best yet, just buy your product or service right there on the spot.

- Lead Magnets – something you give away or sell at a low price to get a prospect involved. Special Reports, videos, an interview, an audio, a Consumer Guide all qualify – but regardless of what form it takes – *if done correctly, your lead magnets are powerful selling tools that engage your prospect and move them closer to buying.*

- NOTE: A lead magnet is a sales presentation in disguise. Done correctly... it SELLS. If not, it's ignored and forgotten by someone *who may have done business with you...* if only your copy had been stronger, more engaging and more compelling.

- Email Sales Campaigns – a SERIES OF SALES LETTERS sent via email. Email selling campaigns can be used to reactivate existing clients, make new offers, secure appointments, and create a cash surge practically anytime.

- Direct Marketing Sales Campaigns – A complete selling strategy to reach your IDEAL PROSPECTS and deliver your STRONGEST MESSAGE. May include sales letters, post-cards,

WHAT MAKES PERSUASIVE SALES COPY – PERSUASIVE

information sheets, consumer guides, special reports, and audio and video elements. Direct marketing is perfect to sell BIG TICKET products and services.

- Other copy elements that can SELL your product or service may include: Brochures, info-graphics, white-papers, mind-maps, flow charts, and so on.
- Sales Funnel Copy – A 'sales funnel' is a SALES LETTER broken into parts and delivered digitally. Sales funnels range from simple to extremely complex with dozen of copywriting elements ... each of which can engage your prospect and move them closer to buying from you – or bore them to death and send them packing.
- *Strong copy engages prospects. And gives you more sales. Weak copy fails to engage. Wastes money. Wastes time. And gives you fewer sales.*

10 GENIUS STEPS TO BECOME A BETTER WRITER

1. Write.
2. Write more.
3. Write even more.
4. Write more than that.
5. Write when you don't want to.
6. Write when you do.
7. Write when you have something to say.
8. Write when you don't have anything to say.
9. Write every day.
10. Write MORE!

SO WHY DO COPYWRITERS GET PAID SO WELL?

Clayton Makepeace, considered by many to be the greatest living direct response copywriter, explained that publishers pay copywriters well for two reasons.

"First, publishers need money to survive and grow and effective sales copy is the ONLY thing that causes prospects to become customers and customers to send them money.

"And second, effective sales copy is the scarcest resource they have – and in this game, the publisher, (business owner), with the most effective sales copy WINS."

> The difference between POWERFUL SALES COPY written by a pro... and average sales, print ad, or funnel copy written by anyone else... could easily mean seven figures a year in your business. Master Direct Response Copywriter - Russell J. Martino www.ConquestCopywriter.com

If you want to learn more about The Structure Of Persuasion email your request to: Russell@StructureOfPersuasion.com

FINAL THOUGHTS ON BUSINESS BUILDING – PERSUASIVE COPY & SELLING MORE OF YOUR PRODUCT OR SERVICE...

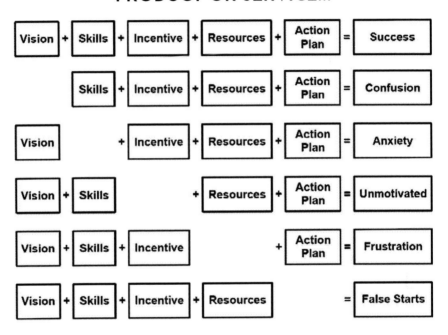

Building a business that keeps customers buying, profit growing and gives you the rewards you want for all the blood, sweat and tears you pour into your business, is no easy task.

The fact is, most businesses fail. And of the ones that survive, most never come close to meeting the owners' expectations for income and wealth accumulation.

Bloomberg reports eight out of ten new businesses, 80%, fail in the first 18-months. And Inc. Magazine reports 96% of all businesses fail sometime in the first ten years.

In his landmark book, *Demystifying Six Sigma*, Alan Larson identifies six primary reasons businesses struggle and fail. Those reasons include, lack of vision, lack of skills, lack of incentive, lack or resources and lack of a strategic action plan.

Larson's chart, (above), is a powerful diagnostic tool you can use to identify the underlying cause responsible for not getting what you want in your business. Since it is impossible to solve a problem without knowing he underlying cause, this is valuable indeed.

EVEN MORE INTERESTING...

After reviewing Larson's chart and considering your business as a whole, evaluate each part of your business *independently* and see how each department stacks up against Larson's criteria.

Say for example, if daily operations run smoothly and you are not forever putting out fires and handling one crisis after another - that means, regarding daily operations;

1. Your vision for the day-to-day operations is clear.
2. You have the skill to get what you want.
3. Your incentive to make day-to-day operations run smoothly is compelling.
4. You have the resources necessary to make day-to-day operations run smoothly.
5. You have an action plan that works.
6. And combined, these factors = success *for that part of your business*.

NOW THINK ABOUT YOUR MARKETING AND SALES PROCESS.

- Do you have systems in place to attract new prospects and get them excited about doing business with you? Or is your

WHAT MAKES PERSUASIVE SALES COPY - PERSUASIVE

marketing hit and miss - with no real strategy to get maximum benefit from every dollar you invest to build your business?

- How effective is your marketing? Do people contact you pre-sold and excited about doing business with you? Or do you have to spend a long time with each prospect, telling each one the same story to get them to buy?
- Do you have an evergreen sales process that can tell your story in an engaging, persuasive manner to an unlimited number of prospects and automatically follow up – so you get maximum value for every dollar you invest in building your business. And so you can focus on attracting new prospects and feeding the automatic sales process, instead of focusing so heavily on closing sales?
- Do your sales messages SELL your product or service? Or is converting a LOOKER into a BUYER and closing sales a time-consuming weak spot you want to improve?

If attracting prospects and closing sales is a weak spot in your business – of if you just want more business because you have the capacity to handle it, then review Larson's chart and ask yourself;

1. Is your VISION, your *step-by-step process* to attract more business and sell a lot more of your product or service, clear?
2. Do you have the MARKETING KNOW HOW and COPYWRITING SKILLS it takes to attract more business and close more sales in-house – or do you need to an outside expert to design effective campaigns, write persuasive copy to get things moving – and then let your team take it from there?
3. Is your INCENTIVE TO ACT strong enough for you to make something happen?

4. Are you determined to sell more, profit more and sock away big chunks of money in an investment or retirement account every year? Or is that commitment half-hearted, more like *'yea that'd be nice'* – instead of – *'Yes, I'm ALL IN. Nothing will stop me. I will not be denied'*. It makes a difference.
5. Are the RESOURCES it takes to get the job done available? Are you willing to commit those resources to reaching your goals?
6. Do you have an ACTION PLAN to reach your sales goals? Do you have a systematic way to attract new business that works? Is your sales message persuasive? Does it convert lookers into buyers?

FULL CIRCLE

After *trying* to sell lighting systems to new car dealers for over a year and failing, Jim sought an outside direct-marketing and copywriting expert to help solve the problem.

He had incentive and the resources to act. But lacked the strategic vision to enter the market. And lacked the know-how and the skill to sell $100k lightning systems to rich car dealers who don't want to be bothered and whose knee-jerk reaction was, the whole idea is crazy.

After acquiring the missing parts... strategic vision, skill to convert and an action plan to guide the process day by day... in less than a year Jim's company became – and still is today - THE DOMINANT FORCE in that market place. *And they've made millions along the way.*

Witness the power of strong direct marketing, persuasive messaging, and CONSISTENTLY getting the RIGHT MESSAGE to the RIGHT MARKET.

WHAT MAKES PERSUASIVE SALES COPY – PERSUASIVE

WHAT'S YOUR NEXT STEP?

Is your marketing & advertising costing you a fortune - instead of making you one?

THE FORTUNE NOT MADE ON BUSINESS NOT DONE IS REAL...

By Master Copywriter & Direct Marketing Expert Russell Martino
Copyright 2017 All Rights Reserved

Marketing and advertising that generates few leads and few sales *costs you exactly the same* as marketing & advertising that gives you a truck load of leads, sales and profit.

Most marketing and advertising is only marginally effective – and dramatically underperforms *compared to what can be done with the same marketing dollars.*

How much has the fortune not made on business not done cost you so far?

EXAMPLE 1:

An obesity surgery center ran radio ads for 3 months with- out booking a single surgery. The new direct response radio ads I wrote generated $108,000 in elective surgery, completed, paid for in cash with money in the bank, in just over 12 weeks.

The media cost to run the WINNING and the LOSING ads was identical.

WHAT MAKES PERSUASIVE SALES COPY – PERSUASIVE

The original ads produced few leads and no new business. The new ads produced dozens of leads and $108,000 in completed business.

Over the first 12 weeks, non-responsive advertising had cost the company

$108,000 in sales-not-made & profit-not-realized on business-not-done.

What kind of ads do you run? Radio? TV? Banner Ads Online? Valpak? Post Cards? Direct Mail? Brochures? Long Form Sales Letters? Social Media? Offline Only? Offline to Online? Online Only?

How effective are your ads? How many leads do they generate? How many sales do they produce? How does one marketing effort compare to another in your business. Which ones give you the best return?

If you can't answer these questions you are shooting in the dark, flying blind, and gambling with your marketing dollars... instead of using them to methodically build your business to the size you want.

Peter Drucker taught, "If you can't measure it, you can't manage it."

Being able to measure response and know how many leads and sales a marketing/advertising effort produces is one reason direct response marketing is so powerful. You know where every lead and every sale comes from. And you know your return on every advertising dollar spent.

EXAMPLE 2:

Another client, a doctor with a $5000 pain treatment pro- gram, was spending $14,000 a month to run a full page ad in the Houston Chronicle. Each month the ad produced a small profit.

The new ad I wrote set the switch board on fire with over 100 phone calls in three days resulting in 40 scheduled appointments and over $100,000 in *actual paid business*.

Five weeks later the doctor ran the ad again with similar results. The ROI for those two ad runs was better than 12 to 1.

FYI - Three years later the doctor was still running the ad every 5 to 9 weeks. And it still getting great results.

Over the first year alone the ads brought $350,000 *more* in completed business than the advertising it replaced.

For this professional practice on that ad campaign, *the-fortune-not-made on business-not-done* was $350,000 a year. *Money now realized!*

How effective are your lead generation systems? Do they deliver you a steady stream of people excited and ready to do business?

Imagine investing the same marketing dollars you do now, but enjoying a 50% or 100% or 250% increase in response. What would that do for your bottom line?

Your answer is part of what you miss out on by not having a stronger message and *more*, or *more effective*, lead generation systems in place working for you 24/7 and 365.

The fortune-not-made on business-not-done is not just an idea. It's a discussion of REAL money. Money that could have been used to grow your business, upgrade your lifestyle or feed your retirement account.

This is as real as it gets.

How much has the *fortune-not-made* on *business-not-done* cost you over the last year? $150,000? $250,000? $500,000? A million? Two million? More?

How much will it cost you over the next year if you don't act now to plug holes in your revenue stream, strengthen your sales message and put a strategy in place to ensure you get MAXIMUM results for every dollar you invest to build your business?

WHY MOST MARKETING & ADVERTISING – EVEN DIRECT RESPONSE MARKETING & ADVERTISING – UNDERPERFORMS

First, if you're not doing direct response advertising, you are wasting money. An average direct response ad will outperform a 'brilliant' award-winning image ad every time.

A good direct response copywriter working from home in his (or her) underwear can write a sales message that, when delivered to the right prospects, will sell circles around anything a fancy New York Ad Agency with a team of 'creatives' and an army of 'award-winning' graphic artists can produce.

And by the way... if you happen to run one of those award-winning agencies... and care to have a friendly little contest, split-testing your entire agency against my copywriting ... by all means, just give me a call.

Now with that said and my testosterone under control... let's get down to business.

PRIMARY REASONS WHY MOST MARKETING & ADVERTISING, INCLUDING DIRECT RESPONSE MARKETING & ADVERTISING, UNDERPERFORMS;

1. The message is weak. Limp. Lackluster. Boring. Lacks authority. Is all about image with no substance. Makes claims with no proof. Focuses on the company, product or spokesperson and not the prospects' fears, concerns, wishes, wants, needs or desires. Fails to mention almost EVERYTHING a prospect may care about. - And because of these problems, (anyone of which is enough to slaughter your response), the message has a tiny impact compared to what can be done.

OR;

2. The message is loud. Abrasive. Hyperbolic. Overbearing. Braggadocios. In-your-face. Unbelievable. Insulting. Threatening. Or so far over the top it would offend an ex-con biker carrying a Glock and a shotgun.

STRUCTURAL REASONS WHY MOST MARKETING & ADVERTISING UNDERPERFORMS;

- The message fails to connect with prospects.
- It fails to hold attention.
- It is disorganized.
- It's weak not strong.
- It fails to engage emotion.
- It fails to demonstrate believable authority.
- It fails to present an air-tight, rock-solid, logical sales argument.
- It fails to detail how much the prospect suffers now... and fails to detail how much better their life will be when they have your product or service.
- It fails to distinguish you from your competitors.
- It fails to get the prospect to realize that YOU and YOU ALONE understand them and can help them get what they want.
- It fails to respect the prospect's intelligence.
- It fails to make an offer, or makes a weak offer instead of a strong irresistible one.
- It fails to reverse the risk.
- It fails to make a call to action with clear instructions on what to do next and what to expect after they do it.
- It fails to create urgency.
- If fails to give people a good reason to click, call or come by now.

WHAT MAKES PERSUASIVE SALES COPY - PERSUASIVE

- It's a structural train wreck that lacks key elements that make direct response copy thought provoking, memorable and persuasive.

HOW EFFECTIVE IS YOUR MESSAGE?

Do your messages hold your prospects attention? Do they get excited? Are your prospects riveted? Do they read every word? Do they respond? Contact you? Buy?

Does your message get your prospects to see your product as THE solution to their problem, the best way to get what they want?

Does your sales message make your prospects feel like they'd have to be crazy to not do business with you?

Does your message *convert lookers into buyers*?

The better your message connects with your prospects the more business you do.

Example: A Houston law firm losing business to competitors asked for help. They were sending about 50 letters a week to prospective clients. But due to competition, the letters, which once worked well, were pulling in fewer clients.

The problem was not competition. The problem was the message. It was 100% company-focused. It didn't stand out. It sounded like every competitors letter. All about the esteemed law firm proudly serving clients for 25 years. And so on.

I trashed the stuffy lawyer letter and replaced it with a 4-page Special Report printed on BRIGHT YELLOW PAPER that got noticed.

When the message and how it showed up changed, the results changed.

The new Report on bright yellow paper with the controversial title - *Tricks & Traps Insurance Companies Use To Cheat Accident Victims Out Of Their Lawful Settlement* – brought in 500% more business every week than the original letter. This resulted in over $2 million in attorney fees net to the law firm over the next 18 months.

The lead partner in the firm calculated that not going to stronger direct response marketing years sooner had cost the firm millions of dollars.

This is another example of *the-fortune-not- made on business-not-done*.

How does this apply to you?

How effective is your marketing? How much better could it be?

How much is your fortune-not-made on business-not-done. What can you do to not miss that business and make those sales?

What's one easy step you could take? Will you take it? When?

MOST MARKETING & ADVERTISING COMMITS ONE OR MORE OF THESE RESPONSE-SLAUGHTERING SALES-KILLING PROFIT-ROBBING MISTAKES...

If your marketing is plagued with even one of these profit-killers you are *bleeding profit* and don't even know it.

You work too hard to miss business that can easily be yours.

Your costs are too high and your risks are too great to get anything less than maximum benefit for every dollar you invest in your marketing.

Don't let these profit-killing mistakes rip the heart out of your money-making potential.

PROFIT-KILLING MISTAKE #1

Wrong Message: Most advertising is company or product-focused, not customer-focused.

WHAT MAKES PERSUASIVE SALES COPY - PERSUASIVE

No one cares about logos, slogans, jingles or pictures of a building a dog or a duck. You know this for a fact because YOU don't depend on those things to make buying decisions.

No one cares about awards you've won, how great your employees are, how you always put your customers first, or about how long you've been in business.

Your customers assume you are in business. They assume you're good at what you do. And they assume you will appreciate their business. You get all that carte blanche.

If all your sales letters, brochures and Web copy do is drone on about 'quality, service and dependability' - you sound exactly like everyone else making the same shallow, self-serving claims anyone with any product can make.

And if you sound like everyone else, YOUR MESSAGE HAS MADE YOU A COMMODITY, where the only thing that matters is price.

- A strong message distinguishes you from your competitors. With the right message, people will drive past a dozen competitors, stand in line and pay more to do business with you... because the right message demonstrates you understand them. And demonstrates you have a superior solution that is perfect for them.
- A strong message establishes your authority in a credible way... *and presents an air-tight sales argument for doing business with you.*
- A strong message details the problems your prospects face because they don't have your product or service – and explains how their life will better when they do.

Why is weak advertising so common?

Weak advertising is common because they are not created by people direct marketing – MAKE A SALE NOW – experience.

Most ads are created by talented graphic artists with off-the-chart design skills but no direct marketing experience... or by advertising sales people - who are skilled at selling advertising - but have no training, no experience and no idea how to create persuasive direct response advertising... that grabs attention and gets people excited and ready to buy.

PROFIT-KILLING MISTAKE #2

Weak Copy: Having weak copy that fails to engage the prospect, fails to hold attention, fails to stimulate emotion, and fails to sell, is a terrible mistake that can cost you a fortune.

The purpose of direct response sales copywriting is to SELL SOMETHING NOW.

In other words, copywriting, *(to quote John E. Kennedy speaking to Albert Lasker in 1905),* is "SALESMANSHIP in PRINT."

Direct response copywriting is not about telling stories, although stories may be told.

It's not about describing the product, although the product may be described.

And it's not about how great the company is, although that may be discussed.

Direct response copywriting and advertising is about SELLING. And in order to sell, you need strong copy that connects with your prospects and presents a case so compelling, your prospect WANTS to do business with you, and feels like it's THEIR idea.

The difference between strong copy and average copy, is like the difference between a top sales pro who sells every day - and an average chump who sells just enough to not get fired.

WHAT MAKES PERSUASIVE SALES COPY - PERSUASIVE

Weak copy is like weak coffee or powdered eggs or bland oatmeal. Or like a timid salesman who will talk forever about kids or football, but is scared to death to ask for the order.

And by the way, STRONG copy does not mean braggadocios, over the top, loud, or in your face. Strong copy feels like a conversation with a friend - who understands what you want, understands the pain of not having it - and has a solution you come to see as 'perfect'.

One problem you face in evaluating your copy needs and deciding if you should write your own copy, or work with a pro is...

YOU DON'T KNOW WHAT YOU DON'T KNOW.

So unless you know *what makes great copy great* - and have experience writing high-octane copy that sells, you have no standard to measure one piece of copy against another.

And even if you recognize great copy the second you see it...

Recognizing great copy does not magically convey the ability to write it any more than recognizing Itzhak Perlman is a great violinist - gives you the ability to pick up his violin and leave audiences spellbound in Carnegie Hall.

PROFIT-KILLING MISTAKE # 3

Not recognizing EVERY Touch-Point is a selling opportunity & every piece of copy is a business asset with the potential to deliver extraordinary value for years.

FROM A SALES PERSPECTIVE...

Sales letters, email marketing campaigns, funnel copy, evergreen sales presentations, lead magnets, audios, videos, white papers, Web copy and so on are tools. Sales tools.

Their only purpose is to engage your prospect. Get you on their radar. Answer questions. Get them excited about what you can do for them. And make a sale.

Having the right tool makes the job easier.

So if your sales letters, Web copy, special reports, email marketing campaigns and so on are not converting as well as you'd like, better tools may be the answer.

FROM A BUSINESS OWNER PERSPECTIVE...

Sales letters, marketing campaigns and so on, are BUSINESS ASSETS capable of generating leads, telling your story and making sales 24/7 and 365.

A good sales letter can sell more of what you sell, including high-ticket products and professional services, in a shorter time than a team of top-gun sales pros ever could.

An effective evergreen sales funnel can deliver your message to more good prospects in a day than a dozen full-time sales people can in a month.

Strong copy is a powerful tool that gives you a HUGE business-building advantage.

Archimedes said, *"Give me a lever long enough and a fulcrum on which to place it, and I shall move the world."*

> Strong copy - and getting that copy in front of good prospects - is the only lever and fulcrum you need to skyrocket sales and reach your goals.

Copywriting elements that support direct marketing strategies include;

WHAT MAKES PERSUASIVE SALES COPY – PERSUASIVE

- A Master Sales Presentation to engage your prospects. Tell your story. And get them to *WANT* to do business with *YOU*. Your Master Presentation can take the form of a long-from sales letter delivered offline *and/or* online, a video sales letter, Magalog, Special Report, audio, script for in-person sales or selling on stage.
- Strong Web Copy to engage prospects and lead them through an Invisible Sales Process that results in action. They join your list. Download a special report. Watch a video. Call you. Email you. Fill out a form. Set an appointment. Or just buy your product or service right there on the spot.
- Lead Magnets – something you give away or sell to get a prospect involved. Special Reports, videos, an interview, an audio, a Consumer Guide all qualify – but regardless of what form it takes – *done correctly, your lead magnets are powerful selling tools that engage your prospect and move them closer to buying.*
- Email Sales Campaigns – a SERIES OF SALES LETTERS sent via email. Email selling campaigns can be used to reactivate existing clients, make new offers, secure appointments, and create a cash surge practically anytime.
- Direct Marketing Sales Campaigns – A complete selling strategy to reach your IDEAL PROSPECTS and deliver your STRONGEST MESSAGE. May include sales letters, post-cards, information sheets, consumer guides, special reports, and audio and video elements. May be offline only, offline to online or online only. Direct marketing campaigns are perfect to sell big-ticket products and services.
- Other copy elements that can SELL your product or service may include: Brochures, info-graphics, white-papers, mind-maps, flow charts, and so on.

- Sales Funnel Copy – A 'sales funnel' is a SALES LETTER broken into parts and delivered digitally. Sales funnels range from simple to extremely complex with dozens of copywriting elements ... each of which can engage your prospect and move them closer to buying from you – or bore them to death and send them packing.

> More than any other factor... the strength of your message to connect with and motivate prospects to do business with you determines how much you sell.

Of course you need good prospects to see your message.

But you can run 10 full-page newspaper ads a day... or get a million page views a day on your Web site... *and without a strong message that captures attention, distinguishes you from competitors and gets people to WANT what you sell and WANT to get it from YOU... you have nothing.*

Cutting corners on your message, which is the only thing that can compel a prospect to buy from you... is a mistake that will cost you a fortune in *'business not done'* over time.

Investing in great copywriting is not only smart, it may be the best investment you can make to keep your doors open, your employees paid... and to ensure the highest return possible on every dollar you invest in marketing, advertising and building your business.

Now, armed with powerful new insight, and confident you have the secret to sell more of whatever you sell than ever before... let's go to the next page!

THE MOST POWERFUL SELLING TOOL ON EARTH... AND HOW TO USE IT TO GROW YOUR BUSINESS

by Master Copywriter & Direct Sales Expert Russell Martino

> Nothing makes a job easier than having the right tool. In this chapter you discover how 'having the right tool brought a start-up manufacturer $200 million+ in sales over 18-months & how you can use the same tool and the same marketing strategy in your business.

My first big-ticket sales job was selling machines that extract liquid natural gas from flowing gas wells at the well head.

Revenue from sale of the liquid natural gas was shared between the well owner, the equipment manufacturer and investors who purchased the machines.

The machines cost $70,000 each.

Being new to sales and clueless about how to sell expensive equipment, I followed the owner's advice on how to sell, which was…

Never try to sell anything to anybody. *Just present the facts, tell the whole story, and let people decide if what you've got is right for them.*

The story behind these machines is fascinating and complex. And since a confused mind never buys, it was important the whole story was told and told well.

To make that happen the company invested in the creation of a selling tool that guaranteed every prospect would get the whole story with nothing left out and all questions answered.

This tool made selling so easy. And transformed a start-up company with an expensive product - into a multi-million dollar enterprise practically overnight.

The tool was a powerful documentary-style sales presentation that educated the viewer on every aspect of the project. You met top management. You got a video tour of the manufacturing facility. You saw welders welding, workers working and machines loaded on 18-wheeler pulling away from the loading dock.

You saw the machines on location and in action, extracting liquid natural gas, which was piped into huge storage tanks.

A former NASA engineer explained how the machines work. A tax attorney explained the tax benefits. A CPA explained how investors get paid.

The president of the company explained why the offer was limited and why, if this was right for you, it was critical you act now or risk missing out.

Everything was explained in detail, including how to purchase a machine and what to do next if you were interested.

It was a brilliant sales presentation that could sell to even the most sophisticated prospect, regardless of who showed up with the video.

With the video in hand, face to face selling couldn't have been easier.

No razzle-dazzle. No need to build rapport, the video did that for you.

Just show up and ask the prospect to view the video.

WHAT MAKES PERSUASIVE SALES COPY - PERSUASIVE

THE ENTIRE SALES STRATEGY WAS;

1. Show up and ask the prospect to view the video;
2. PUSH PLAY *(This was 30+ years ago so I lugged a portable video player around to make sure the video could be viewed.)*;
3. After the video, the only question was; *"Is this right for you?"*

The video established rapport, told the story, answered questions, handled objection, presented a logical sales argument and pinged enough emotion to get people chomping at the bit to buy as many of these $70,000 machines as they could possibly afford.

Using the *Push Play Sales Strategy*, I sold $560,000 worth of equipment the first month. And $840,000 more the second month.

By having a master sales presentation to answer questions, handle objections and tell a great story to the right people, the company did over $200 million in sales the first 18-months in business.

THE MAGIC IS IN THE MESSAGE

Get the RIGHT MESSAGE to the RIGHT PEOPLE and they end up wanting to do business with you.

Like television, radio or print, video is just a way to deliver a message.

And in the case of the gas machines, the message was a masterpiece.

The master sales presentation on video was perfect for anyone who wanted tax breaks, passive income, relatively low risk and a better than average return on their money.

WHAT CUSTOMERS REALLY WANT...

Rest assured, NO ONE wanted a liquid gas extraction machine. But investors happily shelled millions to buy them. Why?

If they didn't want the machines, what did they want?

See if you agree.

People who purchased the machines...

- Wanted to keep the money they worked hard to earn and not have to pay so much in taxes. This fact made the tax breaks that came with the machines attractive.
- They wanted passive income… so they could make money while they sleep or take a vacation... not just when they locked in the office or chained to a desk.
- They wanted safety and a good return… so their future was secure and they could relax and enjoy a nice lifestyle.
- They wanted to make a smart decision and a great investment… so they would be admired by family and respected by peers.
- They wanted to be part of something more exciting than driving back and forth to the office every day... and owning a machine designed by NASA engineers that put you in the heart of the of one of the most profitable businesses on earth, the oil business, did that for them.
- They wanted a great story to tell. In fact, they wanted a great story to tell that they were part of, and to an extent, helped make possible.

THE COMPANY MADE MILLIONS PRACTICALLY OVERNIGHT ON THE POWER OF THE MASTER SALES PRESENTATION VIDEO AND BECAUSE;

1. Participation was restricted to people with a minimum net worth of one million dollars, which means only people who could afford

WHAT MAKES PERSUASIVE SALES COPY – PERSUASIVE

the product and benefit from the tax breaks ever saw the presentation.

2. The message appealed strongly to anyone with investment capital who valued safety, high-yield, passive income and tax breaks, which is exactly what people who bought the machines wanted.

In other words, they got the RIGHT MESSAGE to the RIGHT MARKET.

The result was over $200 million in sales in 18 months.

Getting the right message to the right people works. This strategy, which is Dan Kennedy Marketing 101, (and is much easier to say than do) can catapult sales for any business in record time, including yours.

Imagine having a message powerful enough to sell $200 million worth of your product or service in a year and a half.

How would that affect your bottom line?

With the right message and todays' technology, you can put more PURE SELLING POWER at your command than was even imaginable, much less available, in the past.

Imagine the sense of freedom you would enjoy being able to deliver your best, high-impact, sales presentation and irresistible offer to an unlimited number of prospects, entirely at their convenience, with no inconvenience whatsoever to you.

Your FIRST step to out-market competitors and develop a stream of people who contact you ready to buy... is to have a master presentation that connects with your prospects on a deep emotional level and gets them excited about doing business with you.

Over $200 million in equipment was sold in 18 months primarily because the company invested the time and money it took to craft that kind of master sales presentation.

Without this caliber of presentation...

Without the complete story being told...

Without unquestioned authority being established...

Without the benefits being clearly explained and objections being handled...

And without the emotional firepower woven in from start to finish...

The video wouldn't have mattered.

The video dramatically extended the company's reach because with it, anyone could deliver a master presentation.

With a strong sales presentation that connects with your prospects on a deep emotional level, you command unprecedented selling power.

Without a great story that connects with prospects, you are essentially nowhere. Just a face in the crowd hawking your wares. Just another voice crying out, *buy from me... because I want you to buy from me.*

Some companies limp along and manage to survive like this. But it's not efficient. Not effective. Not fun. And nowhere near as profitable as the same business would be if the owner was willing to take the road less traveled.

To build a great business you need a great product, you need to tell a great story, and that story needs to be told to a lot of people who will benefit from doing business with you.

The gas machine manufacturer had a great product, told a great story to a lot of the right people and did spectacularly well. In this regard, nothing has changed from then to now.

To break free from the crowd of businesses that sputter along and never give you the kind of payoff you really want, you need a good product, you need a great story to tell and you need to tell it well to a LOT of people who can benefit.

WHAT MAKES PERSUASIVE SALES COPY – PERSUASIVE

QUICK REVIEW...

The magic is in the message. When your message connects with people who want to solve the problems and enjoy the benefits your product provides, they're interested.

When your master-presentation focuses on what your prospects really want, and demonstrates how your product helps them get it, your message is irresistible.

THE ULTIMATE SECRET TO GROW YOUR BUSINESS IS CONSISTENTLY GET THE RIGHT MESSAGE TO THE RIGHT PROSPECTS.

Develop the right message for your product or service.

Systematically get that message in front of the right people.

And there's no limit to what you can accomplish.

- You can grow your business to any size.
- You zoom past competitors and leave them in the dust.
- You finally get the kind of payoff you want for all the time you spend and the blood, sweat and tears you pour into running your business.

CONSISTENTLY get the RIGHT MESSAGE to the RIGHT PROSPECTS and your business explodes with sales and profit. This is what marketing is all about... *the key to the kingdom for every business, including yours.*

With stone-age video technology and no Internet, the gas machine manufacturer; 1) developed the right message; 2) got it to the right people, and did over $200 million in business over 18 short months.

With today's technology and the Internet, they could have done TWICE the business in HALF the time at a QUARTER of the cost. Your advantage is real.

The only question is, will you act on it? And if so... when?

105

WITH THE RIGHT MESSAGE DELIVERED IN AUDIO, VIDEO OR PRINT - ONLINE OR OFFLINE;

- Your prospects pay attention;
- You put your best foot forward;
- You build strong rapport with your prospect;
- Your story is engaging and compelling;
- You hold your prospect's interest;
- You establish authority;
- You say something that makes a real difference for your prospect;

THE RIGHT MESSAGE;

- Demonstrates you understand what your customers really want;
- Connects emotionally;
- Distinguishes you from competitors;
- Lays out the facts;
- Educates your prospects so they understand why your product or service is superior;

THE RIGHT MESSAGE;

- Provides proof;
- Builds desire for your product or service;
- Positions your product as THE solution to a problem they want solved, the best way possible to get what they really want, which is never the product or service; *"In the factory we make cosmetics. In the department store we sell hope."* Max Factor
- Builds a value proposition that simply cannot be ignored;
- Answers questions every serious prospect has;

WHAT MAKES PERSUASIVE SALES COPY – PERSUASIVE

THE RIGHT MESSAGE;

- Handles common objections before they arise;
- Gets prospects to realize what you've got is right for them;
- Gets prospects to realize they are fortunate to have found you;
- Makes a compelling offer;
- Creates a sense of urgency;
- Gives your prospect a good reason to ACT NOW;

THE RIGHT MESSAGE;

- Makes your salespeople instantly more effective;
- Shortens the sales cycle;
- Turns lookers into buyers;
- Makes you a category of one;
- Improves your ROI on every dollar you invest in marketing and advertising;
- Results in prospects who; 1) know who you are; 2) know what you do, and; 3) are excited about doing business with you *before you ever speak with them.*

If your message does not convert like crazy, either you're reaching the wrong people, or the message and/or your offer are simply weak and miss the mark.

It doesn't matter who you are or how successful you are – from multi-millionaire to the newest kid on the block... if you want to sell more of whatever you sell... improve your message, strengthen your offer and tell your story to good prospects more often.

Now, with paper and pen in hand, re-read Part One *What Makes Persuasive Sales Copy Persuasive* and begin applying what you learn to YOUR sales message.

See what you come up with.

You may be surprised at how much better it is than what you've got now.

And if you decide you need some help, reach out.

It's that simple.

WHAT MAKES PERSUASIVE SALES COPY - PERSUASIVE

THE RIGHT MESSAGE FOR YOUR BUSINESS WHAT IT SOUNDS LIKE - WHAT'S YOUR ALTERNATIVE IS GETTING IT RIGHT WORTH THE EFFORT...

by Master Copywriter & Direct Marketing Expert Russell Martino

It makes no difference if you're a multi-millionaire or just getting by.

It doesn't matter what you sell, from big-ticket professional services – to expensive coaching and membership sites - to investments in anything – to fundraising for any cause – to getting tons of free publicity – to selling your ideas or promoting political candidates -- to selling ANY product or service you can name at ANY price point... including the product or service you sell now to earn your living...

Your degree of success, cash-flow, profitability - and whether or not you ever have the kind of life you want most for yourself and your family after you retire... is determined PRIMARILY by your ability to sell your product or service.

And your ability to SELL is determined primarily by;

1. Having THE RIGHT MESSAGE for your market – *so when your message reaches your prospects online or offline, you get their attention. And they're interested.*
2. Having STRONG COPY to engage your prospects, tell your story in a compelling way that holds your prospects attention, demonstrates you understand them - *and builds their desire for your product.*
3. Having an IRRESISTIBLE OFFER – *so when your prospect sees what you have for them, they WANT IT. They WANT IT FROM YOU. And they WANT IT NOW.*
4. CONSISTENTLY getting the RIGHT MESSAGE to the RIGHT PROSPECTS & FOLLOWING-UP ON ALL LEADS – *so you get maximum benefit for every dollar your invest in copy, technology, traffic, advertising and so on.*

YOU KNOW YOUR MESSAGE IS RIGHT & YOUR COPY IS STRONG WHEN...

- You know your MESSAGE IS RIGHT and YOUR COPY IS STRONG - when your prospects ignore competitors and contact you excited and ready to buy.
- You know it's right - when you run a sales campaign, (online or offline), and your response is so high you are delighted - which means you do a lot of business, get a great ROI on your campaign and you get a lot of good leads.
- You know you've got it right - when your EVERGREEN SALES FUNNEL is up and running, tested, proven, converting LOOKERS into BUYERS - and adding to the bottom line each and every day.

WHAT MAKES PERSUASIVE SALES COPY – PERSUASIVE

- You know you've got it right when prospects consume your MASTER SALES PRESENTATION, which may be a sales letter or VSL, a series of videos, a Special Report or Consumer Guide, or an email marketing campaign -- and then do business with you and become your customer, client, patient or patron.
- You know you've got it right - when the ROI on each ad or marketing campaign you run is so OFF THE CHART HIGH.
- You know you've got it right when you have multiple sales channels attracting prospects and feeding leads into your automatic-evergreen-sales-process.
- You know you've got it right when your automatic sales process converts unconverted leads into buyers and delivers you a steady stream of business.

AN INCONVENIENT TRUTH...

There's a disturbing trend in marketing today that's causing the unaware business owner to pony up big out-of-pocket costs that are often wasted. And then costing them a FORTUNE in missed opportunity and business not done.

That trend is to cut corners on message development and copywriting by trying to write copy themselves* - or by using pre-written, canned, one-size-fits-all copy a staff member or junior agency copywriter can *'swipe'* and repurpose to sell the products and services that must be sold for you to prosper.

* NOTE: If you are a proven direct response copywriter with a long list of successful promotions to your credit – and have time to stop running your business for a few weeks and write, congratulations. It's fine to write your own copy.

But if you're not an experienced direct response copywriter with a long string of profitable promotions to your credit...

...in my experience, trying to write your own copy will be a train wreck - an unhappy, aggravating, expensive waste of time that ends with you forgetting the whole thing, biting the bullet and finding a real copywriter.

Trying to write your own copy is like a rich guy buying a pro football team... and deciding to play quarterback. *Ouch!*

ABOUT SWIPED COPY

THE TREND TO USE SWIPED, CANNED, CUT & PASTE COPY IS POPULAR BECAUSE;

1. On the surface canned copy is cheap, especially compared to A-level copywriting that creates a message unique to your business, ideal for your prospects - and is strong enough to actually persuade someone to buy something.

If you don't know or appreciate the difference between strong, original copy, and cut & paste, ticky-tacky copy, it's easy to make the mistake of buying copy based on price alone. *But it's not easy to avoid the consequences.*

The problem is, you get what you pay for.

The difference between canned copy and strong, original copy is huge.

It's like the difference between a cheap TV dinner - and a wonderful gourmet meal at a nice restaurant. If you want to impress someone, *(like a good prospect for your product or service)*, which would you choose?

Canned copy written to be *adapted* to any business is by necessity, common.

Cut-and-paste copy is non-specific, and by necessity, full of vague generalizations and unsubstantiated claims any business can make.

WHAT MAKES PERSUASIVE SALES COPY – PERSUASIVE

This kind of copy makes every businesses sound the same. And that makes you a *'me-too'* advertiser – like any chump hawking wears on any street corner.

The only thing that sets *me-too* advertisers apart from each other is price.

So if you use *me-too*, cut-and-paste copy – *or any copy that fails to captivate your prospects and get them excited about doing business with you* -- be prepared to cut your prices to the bone. Because when your message sounds just like your competitors, price is the only distinguisher you prospects will see.

To *fix* canned copy and make it even marginally acceptable, requires so much rewriting and adaptation by a good copywriter, you're better off investing more right up front and going with a proven direct response copywriter.

Even with rewriting and adaptation, canned copy is not original. It's like a Volkswagen Beetle dressed up with a mail-order kit to look like a Rolls Royce.

It's different. It may hold your attention for a minute or two. But no one takes it seriously for very long. They say *'Isn't that cute.'* And move on.

Another Risk...

Another risk you run using canned, cut & paste copy is, A-level direct response copywriters seldom write copy intended for cut & paste repurposing.

And that means the odds of your nice-sounding, space-filling, swiped copy ever selling anything are low indeed.

The cost of cutting corners on copy can be enormous.

For big-ticket products and services, going with *cheap copy* could cost you hundreds of thousands to over a million dollars a year in missed sales.

This is a *fortune-not-made on business-not-done*. And it's real.

A chain is as strong as its' weakest link.

But without a strong sales message that converts lookers into buyers, every other part of your business can be ROCK SOLID, every chain link at maximum strength... and you'll still miss sales and bleed profit.

On the other side of that coin – in spite of other problems you may have in your business, IF YOUR SALES MESSAGE CONVERTS LOOKERS INTO BUYERS, odds are you will survive, fix the other problems and prosper.

Even if the difference between cut-rate copy and working with a proven direct response copywriter is several hundred percent...

Even if it's the difference is between fifteen hundred and fifteen thousand dollars – or the difference is between $7500 and $75,000 or double that...

If you sell an expensive product or service...

Strong Copy is a capital investment to acquire a business asset that may help your business grow for YEARS, often without changing a word, once the copy is tested and proven.

Strong copy is a one-time investment you may recover with a few sales.

Cutting corners on copy is gambling your future and risking hundreds of thousands of dollars a year in missed profit... to save what is comparatively, just a few pennies.

2. The second reason a business owner may make the mistake of going with cut-rate copy is; **you don't know what you don't know**. So it's easy to make a mistake.

3. If you're not a copy expert - and someone selling copy cheap *sounds like an expert* – you may mistake them for one - and end up buying a cut-rate version of the ONLY THING you should never cut corners on, which is developing the right persuasive message for your business.

WHAT MAKES PERSUASIVE SALES COPY – PERSUASIVE

The RIGHT MESSAGE, STRONG COPY and a GREAT OFFER are what convert lookers into buyers and SELLS your product. Without that, your business is done. *With it, there's no limit on what you can accomplish.*

Not going with the best copy possible is a profit-killing mistake you pay for every day of your life with fewer sales, lower profits and dreams not realized.

Relying on cheap copy to connect with your prospects and sell your product or service is like taking a pocket knife to a gun fight.

It's like starting a high school quarterback in the Super Bowl because he costs less than the all-pro quarterback who went 15 and 1 last season.

It's like tossing a kid in the cage with the reigning MMA freestyle karate champion and expecting anything other than a stone cold slaughter.

It's like trying to cross the Atlantic in a row boat during a category 5 hurricane and expecting to survive.

Cutting corners on the ONLY THING that can keep your business humming, keep people buying and give you a good return on your investment is worse than betting against the odds. It denying reality.

"THE STRONGER YOUR COPY THE MORE YOU SELL"

Strong copy is the ONLY THING that can give you MAXIMUM RETURN for the time, energy, money, blood, sweat and tears you pour into your business.

Technology is important. But the only purpose of technology is to deliver messages. MESSAGES sell your product or service... not the message delivery vehicle.

Technology can help you sell more. But in and of itself, technology sells nothing.

Overspending on technology and underestimating the value of copy is like buying a fleet of expensive mail trucks to deliver junk mail people trash without even opening.

Underestimating the value of copy and cutting corners to save a few bucks guarantees a poor ROI for all the time and money you pour into building your business.

Good marketing is simple.

There are no magic buttons to push. No secrets to reveal. No 'inside information' that makes a dimes worth of difference when it comes to selling.

Consistently get the RIGHT MESSAGE to the RIGHT MARKET and you win. Fail to do that and you lose. It's that simple.

Copywriting is about developing the right message for your market, and presenting that message in a compelling way that gets people excited about doing business with YOU.

In today's ultra-competitive environment consumers have choices. Strong copy makes it clear YOU are the only rational choice to do business with. Because YOU understand.

Average copy attracts your prospects' interest with about the same intensity as students with an average grades attract recruiters looking for top-talent to hire after graduation.

I have never seen average copy do well.

Of course, average copy is be better than nothing. Right?

Or is it?

Average copy can poison the well. Average copy... *focused on the product or service and not the real reasons people buy...* can run off good prospects as fast as you pay for advertising to attract them. *And when they go, they're gone.*

Average copy guarantees fewer people join your list. Fewer learn what you do. Fewer care. Fewer buy. And that means instead of racking up sales or signing up new clients or patients, you're lucky to break even on your marketing.

Why risk it?

Every time I've been engaged to replace weak copy a client got cheap... with strong, A-level, emotion-wrenching copy... results have been quick. Dramatic. And profitable.

YOU CAN'T BAKE A CAKE WITH A SCREWDRIVER...

You need an oven - *not a screwdriver* – to bake a cake.

You need golf clubs - *not a ping-pong paddle* – to play golf.

And to sell a LOT MORE of your product or service... you need strong compelling copy *that grabs your prospects attention- holds their interest - and gets them THRILLED about doing business with you.*

More than any other factor... the strength of your message to connect with and motivate prospects to do business with you... determines how much you sell. How much you earn. And whether or not you stay in business.

Strong, engaging copy focused on what your prospect wants, *which is a RESULT, FEELING or OUTCOME* and not a product or service, will get attention. Build excitement. And convert LOOKERS *who read you're your sales message or view it in the form of a video* - into BUYERS *who give you money.*

Since your business, state of mind, and entire financial-future depend on people *buying your product or service* ... having copy that converts lookers into buyers is critical.

Anything less puts you, your business and your future in *clear and present danger.*

Copywriting is SALESMANSHIP IN PRINT.

Since your standard of living, quality of life and financial future depend on how many people buy your product or service, two things are abundantly clear.

1. Cutting corners on your message, *which is the only thing that can compel a prospect to buy from you...* is a mistake that wastes money, and can cost you a fortune in *'business not done'* over time.

2. Having the BEST COPYWRITING possible, *even if it costs more than you expect*, is not only smart, it may be the SINGLE BEST INVESTMENT you can make to help ensure you receive a great and ongoing return on every dollar you invest to build your business.

This is what GREAT COPY can do for you!

WHAT'S THE RIGHT MESSAGE FOR YOUR BUSINESS & WHAT MAKES THE RIGHT MESSAGE - RIGHT...

The right message GETS NOTICED.

The right message doesn't bang on the door like a maniac. The right message ENTERS THE CONVERSATION going on in the prospects mind.

The right message CONNECTS and HOLDS ATTENTION because the right message is about things IMPORTANT TO YOUR CUSTOMER.

The right message addresses your prospects wants, needs, fears and concerns.

The right message ESTABLISHES YOUR AUTHORITY.

The right message ANSWERS QUESTIONS any customer will have.

The right message HANDLES OBJECTIONS before they come up.

WHAT MAKES PERSUASIVE SALES COPY – PERSUASIVE

The right message demonstrates YOU UNDERSTAND your prospects' situation, you know how they feel and you have the solution that's right for them.

The right massage is never confusing, unbelievable or boring.

The right message demonstrates YOU KNOW what your customers want.

You NEED a drill. But you WANT a hole, because you WANT to display the beautiful painting you bought on a trip to Europe.

You WANT to tell the story of how you acquired that wonderful painting. You WANT to enjoy your friends' reactions when they hear your story and see your beautiful painting hanging majestically in your lovely home.

And it all begins with a drill. But not just any drill. For a job this important the only drill that will do is the ACME Mona Lisa – approved by the Louvre Museum in Paris and the Metropolitan Museum in New York for hanging Master Art Work in homes. Ask for ACME Mona Lisa - the drill you can trust.

The right message IS COMPELLING. *People WANT to respond.*

The right message CREATES A SENSE OF URGENCY.

The right message gives your customer a REASON TO ACT NOW.

The right message tells the prospect what to do now, what to do next and what to expect when they do it.

The right message future paces the prospect and gives them an OWNERSHIP EXPERIENCE by describing how their will life will be better with the product.

The right message offers incentive to ACT NOW.

Get the RIGHT MESSAGE to the RIGHT PEOPLE and you become a CATEGORY OF ONE. Competitors bragging about how great they are, are seen as clueless. *They're all made out of ticky-tacky and all sound just the same.*

With the right message and strong copy that distinguishes you from the herd or me-too marketers... you are recognized as unique - *the only logical choice* to do business with.

Developing the right messages and getting those messages to the right people is what MARKETING is all about. *This is what makes the phone ring. This is what gets people to contact you presold and ready to buy.*

The entire purpose of getting your message right is to *make sales.* Einstein said, "Nothing happens until something moves."

The right message gets things moving.

The right message *converts lookers into buyers.*

The right message makes the cash register ring.

WHY PEOPLE BUY...

When there's a discrepancy between what you want and you've got - it's uncomfortable.

In psychology the *discomfort* you feel when there is a gap between what you have and what you want... is called *cognitive dissonance.*

- If your sales are not what you want, it creates discomfort, or cognitive dissonance.
- If your income is not what you want, it creates discomfort, or cognitive dissonance.
- If you feel like a slave in your business, you suffer with cognitive dissonance.

If anything about your business, *(or life),* is not the way you want, if you're unhappy or dissatisfied, or wish things were different, it creates cognitive dissonance.

WHAT MAKES PERSUASIVE SALES COPY - PERSUASIVE

THE FIX FOR COGNITIVE DISSONANCE IS TO;

1. Blame someone, which doesn't solve a thing but makes you feel better, OR;
2. Do something about it, like change something, *or buy something.*

> Max Factor famously said,
> *"In the lab we make cosmetics, but in the drug store we sell hope."*

Most purchases are like buying cosmetics.

You offer a product or service. But your prospects want solutions and outcomes.

Talk about products and services and you sound just like everyone else.

Talk about problems, solutions and outcomes, and you have their attention.

Explain how your widget closes the gap between what your prospect has and what they want, and they begin to see you as a friend who understands and can help.

- We want affluence - so we buy expensive items, even if we can't afford them.
- We want health - so we buy health club memberships and exercise equipment.
- We want to look good - so we buy designer cloths, expensive shoes and hand over big money for cosmetic surgery and expensive dental procedures.

YOUR PROSPECTS DON'T WANT PRODUCTS OR SERVICES.

Your prospects want feelings, outcomes and results. So they buy products they believe will move them closer to having what they really want.

Products are delivery vehicles.

Copy that drones on about the company and the product is common, weak and not persuasive. Copy all about the prospect - and how they will be healthier, smarter, more respected, richer and better looking after they have your widget - is strong.

SECRETS TO WRITING COPY THAT SELLS

Emotion drives the DESIRE to buy.

Logic drives the DECISION to complete the purchase.

No one *needs* a $60,000 car, yet hundreds of thousands of people buy them every year.

Ask any luxury car owner why they spend 400% more on a car than need be and they'll talk acceleration, transmission, suspension, brakes, advanced safety features, maneuverability, warranty and so on... you'll hear all the logical reasons why their luxury car is easily worth four times more than other perfectly good automobiles that provide equally dependable transportation.

World-class engineering, warp-speed acceleration, life-saving safety features and so on are valuable, *but these factors are not why we buy expensive cars*.

We buy expensive cars for emotional reasons, things like;

- You *like the way you feel* when you drive a fine luxury vehicle;

WHAT MAKES PERSUASIVE SALES COPY – PERSUASIVE

- You *like the way you look* behind the wheel, which easily justifies the Corinthian leather, the space age dash and the eleven-coat paint job with NASA approved paint sealer;
- You work hard and *feel like you deserve* a fine automobile;
- An expensive car *distinguishes you* as someone who appreciates the finer things in life;
- An expensive car *identifies you as successful*, classy, conservative, fun-loving, powerful or sexy depending on the make and model;
- An expensive car may bestow a *feeling of confidence or superiority*;
- An expensive car says *I can have whatever I want* and this proves it;
- An expensive car *gets you recognized* without having to say a word;
- An expensive car *puts you in an unique club* of other expensive car owners and separates you from those nice, but ineffective people, who can't make the grade;
- An expensive car *impresses people* and *gets you recognition* you may not get otherwise;
- An expensive car tells the world *you want the best* and are *willing and able to pay for it*;
- An expensive car means you've *escaped financial worry* and *live life on your own terms*;
- An expensive car may be a *symbol* that reminds you hard work has rewards;
- An expensive car may represent *freedom to express yourself* exactly as you choose;
- An expensive car is *a joy to drive*, and you like feeling joyful;

This list goes on, but the point is made. We buy expensive cars for EMOTIONAL reasons and justify the purchase with LOGICAL reasons. *And so it is with everything.*

In face-to-face sales and in copy – which is salesmanship in print - emotion and logic make the world go around. One without the other fails.

- Fail to engage your prospect emotionally and they'll ignore your sales message like it wasn't there. *Alas, the perils of weak copy!*
- Fail to provide a strong, logical sales argument for purchasing - and your emotionally engaged prospect simply won't buy. They'll like it. They'll want it. *But they won't pull the trigger.*

Engage emotion by asking questions and determining what your prospect wants to accomplish or avoid.

Anything your prospect wants to move toward or away from is an emotional issue. The stronger their desire to move toward or away from, the stronger the emotions involved.

Develop interest by demonstrating your product as the right tool... or the solution to help your prospect get what they want or avoid what they don't want.

Seal the deal by presenting a logical sales argument that is on-track with your prospects needs, wants, values and buying criteria. When your copy accomplishes this... and you make an irresistible offer... people will leap and lunge to buy your product.

With the right message and a consistent way to get that message in the hands of the right people... you can sell more than ever. Earn more than ever. And secure your future with greater certainty than ever.

- Your message can be positioned in many ways. You're not restricted to just one.

WHAT MAKES PERSUASIVE SALES COPY – PERSUASIVE

- Your message can take the form of an informative webinar, or interview with you the expert, offering advice and answering questions.
- Your message can take the form of s Special Report or Consumer Guide that establishes your authority. And explains what to look for and look out for when considering your kind of product or service.
- Your message can take the form of a revealing documentary or expose explaining problems and the dire consequences of not solving them.

Regardless of your business, profession, product or service; from A to Z, get the RIGHT MESSAGE to the RIGHT PROSPECTS and people will contact you ready to do business.

THE MAGIC IS IN THE MESSAGE.

The secret to grow your business is CONSISTENTLY get the RIGHT MESSAGE to the RIGHT PROSPECTS.

Without the RIGHT MESSAGE, nothing else matters because nothing happens.

Without the right message, slick brochures are a waste of money.

Fail to develop the RIGHT MESSAGE or fail to CONSISTENTLY get the RIGHT MESSAGE to THE RIGHT PEOPLE - and as good as your sales material may look, you'll be lucky if you ever sell a thing.

> The RIGHT MESSAGE scribbled on scratch paper in crayon, delivered to the RIGHT PROSPECTS... will ALWAYS give you MORE SALES and MORE PROFIT than any fancy brochure or slick ad campaign ever could.

NEVER CONFUSE MESSAGE WITH IMAGE.

Growing a business has nothing to do with graphically beautiful Web sites, slick advertising or fancy brochures that deliver company-focused messages.

GROWING A BUSINESS IS A STRAIGHT-FORWARD PROCESS.

Develop the right message for your product or service. And then get the RIGHT MESSAGE to the RIGHT PEOPLE and your business grows.

Do that consistently… and the sky is the limit.

Fail to get the RIGHT MESSAGE to the RIGHT PEOPLE and a million dollars a day in slick advertising won't save you.

If you don't believe this, just ask the former CEOs of any one of dozens of companies that vanished in thin air after spending tens of millions of dollars on national advertising, including Super Bowl commercials.

The commercials won awards.

The agencies that produced them patted themselves on the back.

And the companies went broke, because as entertaining as the messages were, spending money is serious business.

Commercials may be entertaining. Brochures and Web sites may beautiful. *So what!*

If you want my money, you better give me a darn good reason to give it to you. And odds are you, and everyone you want to do business with, are the same.

So if you want your prospects to trust you, do business with you and give you money, you better give them a darn good reason to shell out their hard-earned cash.

This is what developing the right message is all is about. *Giving your prospect such good reasons to do business with you and give you money... they gladly hand it over!*

WHAT MAKES PERSUASIVE SALES COPY - PERSUASIVE

With a good product, strong copy and a superior marketing strategy there is NO LIMIT to what you can accomplish and no limit to how much you can earn.

A good product, strong copy and superior marketing strategy are the best *business-building, wealth-building,* and *securing-the-future* tools anyone can have.

IS IT WORTH THE EFFORT?

That's a question only you can answer.

WHAT IT TAKES TO TRANSFORM YOUR BUSINESS INTO A HIGH-POWERED WEALTH-BUILDING MONEY-MAKING MACHINE...

Here's what I discovered. Grab what you like. Save the rest for later.

> "We all suffer from one of two pains. The pain of discipline or the pain of regret. The difference is discipline weights ounces, while regret weights tons." - Jim Rohn
>
> "The truth behind nearly all successful people is hard work." - Dan Kennedy

1 - CLARITY OF PURPOSE:

Clarity is a choice, not an accident or a gift. Without conscious and directed action on your part, your business will just drift along.

How do you rate yourself on clarity of purpose? Top of the chart? Or still working on it?

Is where you are today, where you thought you'd be three years ago?

Do you have a clear vision for your business going forward? Do you have daily goals, weekly, monthly, quarterly and annual goals? Do you have a three year plan?

Do you have a strategic plan to reach your goals?

What can you do differently to reach your goals sooner rather than later? More importantly, what WILL you do to reach your goals sooner?

2 – DIRECT RESPONSE MIND SET:

If you're not using direct response marketing, you're just twiddling your thumbs and wasting precious time.

'Build it and they will come' is a great movie theme about ghost baseball players... but 'build it and they will come' is a disparately misguided marketing approach.

If you want more business, the process is simple. REACH OUT AND TOUCH SOMEONE! Identify your best prospects. Create DIRECT RESPONSE marketing campaigns to get their attention. Have STRONG copy that converts. Test campaigns to prove they work. POUR IT ON! And deliver. *That's how to build a business.*

3 – CLEAR UNDERSTANDING OF WHAT YOUR CUSTOMERS REALLY WANT – HOW YOUR PRODUCT GIVES IT TO THEM – AND WHY THEY'D HAVE TO BE CRAZY TO NOT GET IT FROM YOU:

Discussed in every chapter in this book. Priceless information!

4- PERSUASIVE COPY THAT CONNECTS WITH YOUR PROSPECTS AND GETS THEM TO WANT TO DO BUSINESS WITH YOU:

Discussed in every chapter.

5 – STRATEGIC PLAN:

"Tactics without strategy is the noise before defeat." Sun Tzu

WHAT MAKES PERSUASIVE SALES COPY - PERSUASIVE

6 - OPTIMUM OPERATING CAPACITY AS A GOAL:

Optimum operating capacity is the amount of business you can do without additional capital investment – and without driving everyone crazy because you're so busy. Think of it a bandwidth.

How much MORE business can you handle without buying equipment, hiring employees or needing a larger facility?

After you meet fixed costs, a big percentage of every dollar you take in - moving toward optimal operating capacity – goes straight to the bottom line.

Reaching your Optimal Operating Capacity is a great goal. And a recipe for profit.

7 - EVERGREEN SELLING SYSTEMS:

Evergreen selling systems are a great way to reach and maintain your Optimal Operating Capacity because you can control the process.

Having an Evergreen Selling System for your core product or service built, tested, proven, in place and working – puts your hand on THE PROFIT THROTTLE. You can throttle-up and generate a flood of business anytime you like. Or throttle-back to a slow trickle – until you're ready to pour it on again.

An Evergreen Selling System that works is a powerful business-building asset.

With a strong sales message and an evergreen selling system in place to deliver that message and automatically follow up with leads... you can scale your business to any size and grow as fast as you want.

A good evergreen selling system can get your sales message in front of more good prospects in a week than a dozen sales people working twelve hours a day can in a month. And that's not even a slight exaggeration.

With a strong sales message, the right technology, and the ability to get people to your sales message... a small company can SELL CIRCLES around much bigger competitors.

CAUTION: Don't be seduced by technology. Technology is important. But with the wrong sales message – you can blow a million dollars on technology and never sell a thing. Technology DELIVERS MESSAGES. Strong copy SELLS.

8 – A STEADY STREAM OF LEADS FROM MULTIPLE LEAD SOURCES

Direct mail, radio, television, print media, organic traffic, pixel marketing, JVs, affiliates, PR, referral, host-beneficiary, automated internal marketing... and so on.

9 – A CLEAR STRATEGY TO;

a) make more new sales;

b) increase the frequency of purchase from existing customers; and;

c) raise the average transaction size of a purchase without just raising the price.

WHAT'S MOST IMPORTANT?

I'll leave that for you to answer. My thoughts are simply this...

If you get EVERYTHING on this list PERFECT ... *except strong copy that connects with your prospects, holds attention and converts lookers into buyers...* you have nothing.

With strong copy, the right technology, and a little marketing know-how, the only questions are; How big do you want to grow? And how fast do you want to go.

Your questions and comments are welcome. And I'm happy to discuss your copy needs.

WHAT MAKES PERSUASIVE SALES COPY – PERSUASIVE

You can reach me by email at Russell@ConquestCopywriter.com or leave a message on my 24-hour message service at 281-487-5876.

SECRETS OF PIXEL MARKETING REVEALED

How to Get Your Sales Message in Front of
Thousands of Good Prospects Every Week
For Pennies Each – A Special Report
By Brian Hahn CEO, GoSocialExperts.com

> Nothing else that you can do in marketing will bring you as many sales as fast and inexpensively as Pixel Marketing. In this chapter you're going to discover how a company routinely sells a $1,644 training program that you have to pack up your RV and travel 100's of miles to participate in using Pixel Marketing. You'll be able to use this same strategy in your business.

One of our long-term clients has a product they sell that teaches people how to repair and maintain their own RV's (Recreational Vehicle). You may not know that over 80% of all RV problems can be solved by an RV owner as long as they know how the systems in their RV work.

If you happen to be one of these owners and you have an expensive vehicle/home that you want to enjoy, this course could save you $1,000's of dollars and possibly salvage a trip.

WHAT MAKES PERSUASIVE SALES COPY – PERSUASIVE

The challenge is that to participate in this live course you have to travel to where the course is being held in your RV so that you can practice on your own unit.

The course does rotate around the country, but this is still quite a commitment for the participants.

To make this more remarkable, we are using pixel marketing which takes place on the internet. While they do have a phone number you can call with questions, most of the sales come through their website.

So, what kind of results do they get?

They average between 5 and 10 sales a month while only spending $600 per month on advertising.

That is $8,220 to $16,440 per month in sales from an ad spend of only $600, or put another way a 13.7X to 27.4X return on their ad spend.

So what is pixel marketing you ask?

What is the magic that lets this company and many others get these kinds of results?

It is the ability for you to tag or mark anyone who comes to your website with a pixel, and then show them ads while they are on other websites.

It is also called remarketing or retargeting.

It gives you, the advertiser, the ability to reach out and follow up with the people that have come to your website or a specific webpage, even if they haven't given you any of their contact information.

This may help explain it.

Imagine you're in your car driving down the highway and you see a billboard for a new Audi. Now your conscious mind may or may not recognize this yet, but . . .

A few minutes later you hear a commercial on the radio for that Audi.

And then when you get home there is a postcard in your mailbox from the local Audi dealer.

And when you're watching the news later that night you see an ad for the newest Audi.

While we can't accomplish this in the physical world yet, we can do this online.

This ability to reach out again and again to people who have done something to express interest in your product or service is what makes pixel marketing so powerful.

After all, no one is going to random websites by just clicking on them. If someone is on your website they have an interest in what you sell.

Once you know that this person has visited your website you can reach out to them again and again possibly with the same message, maybe with other messages.

This lets you concentrate your ad investments on people who have expressed an interest in your products and services.

Having this ability to talk to people who have expressed an interest in what you do, not only by what they say, but by what they DO is what makes the results so incredible.

Now, one question that I get asked when I get to this point is how do these people find out about your website in the first place?

Do people have to get to your site from one particular traffic source?

The answer, no, they can come to your website from any traffic source.

As we work with Facebook marketing we like to recommend that you use Facebook to send a wider audience to your site, and it is a powerful strategy, but it doesn't have to be Facebook that gets people to your site.

It can be:
1. Organic traffic (someone Google showed your site to in a search)
2. Direct traffic (someone who typed in your site's address)

WHAT MAKES PERSUASIVE SALES COPY – PERSUASIVE

3. Newspaper ads (directing readers to go to your website)
4. Postcard
5. Sales Letter
6. Sales Brochure
7. Radio
8. TV
9. Speaking at an event
10. A booth at an event
11. Networking meeting
12. Google Ad words
13. Social Media post or update
14. Link in an email
15. And any other means you can think of to get people to your website.

As you can see there are many ways you can get people to your website, and you're undoubtedly using some of these now.

The question is "Are you set up to take FULL advantage of this traffic"?

Are you pixeling people and if you are, are you reaching back out to them?

Some people think they are pixel marketing but see no results.

What is happening?

These are the top three mistakes we find when talking to potential clients.

FIRST, IS NOT SETTING UP THE PIXEL ON YOUR WEBSITE.

There is a tool that is a chrome extension called the Facebook Pixel Helper.

This tool shows if there is a Facebook pixel on any website you go to. It can be your site or any website you are on. It's amazing to me how many websites don't have a pixel on them.

Facebook can't start gathering data for you until you put the pixel on your site. You don't have to use it right away. Facebook will keep these people in an audience for you for up to 180 days and you can reach out to them, however, you can only go back as far as the day you put the pixel on your site.

THE SECOND MISTAKE I SEE BEING MADE IS NOT DOING ANYTHING WITH THE AUDIENCE YOU'RE GENERATING.

Often, when people come to us for help they have the pixel set up on their site, but they're not doing anything with it.

Now it's great that they have the data the pixel gathered for us to work with, but they missed months of possible sales increases by waiting.

Also, the longer you wait to reach out to a web visitor after they were on your site the less likely it is that they will buy from you or even remember you.

Can you remember every site you visited in the last 180 days? I know that I can't.

So while we have the data to use, there were a number of sales that got missed by not utilizing the data sooner.

The other issue we see is people not considering how they can grow their pixeled audience.

If in everything you do, you think about how to get more people to your website, you're going to see your traffic explode and this will give you more people to work with.

We see potential clients not planning on sending people to their websites when they are developing an offline campaign.

WHAT MAKES PERSUASIVE SALES COPY - PERSUASIVE

Campaigns that are completely offline work, but many times you can multiply the results be adding an online component to the same campaign, and it doesn't have to be complex to make this happen.

THE THIRD MISTAKE I SEE BEING MADE IS POOR MESSAGING.

Once you have the pixel in place and are building your audience, you want to be reaching out to these people.

The difference in your messaging with these types of ads vs. ads going to a wider audience is that these people are familiar with you.

You talk to a longtime friend differently than someone you've known a few months and you talk to this person differently than you do someone you just met, and the person you just met is different from a stranger.

The first ads you're running that you've designed to bring people to your website have one type of language and offer.

When you're reaching out to someone that already came to your site, you must use a different type of language.

After all, you know each other now and are developing your relationship.

As you can see pixel marketing can be a powerful tool to add to your marketing arsenal.

Add it to all your marketing campaigns and start watching your results improve.

I've set aside some time for the readers of this book on my schedule.

You can go to www.gosocialexperts.com/callbrian45 to schedule a time for a Complimentary Facebook Pixel Marketing Session.

We will go over what you're doing now for marketing and how you can add Pixel Marketing to your sales efforts. When we're done you'll have a plan outlined that you can implement or if you want we can help you implement, so that you too can be a Facebook Marketing success.

For more information on a complete online Facebook marketing program go to www.gosocialexperts.com/masterclass. This is a 5 video FREE training program that will show you what a complete Facebook marketing program looks like.

For more information about Brian you can go to www.gosocialexperts.com/about, and yes when you're there you will be pixeled. I do practice what I teach.

Have a great day!

CONVERTING COPY INTO CASH
A SPECIAL REPORT...

by Parthiv Shah – Co-Founder of eLaunchers.com

Converting copy into cash is not as easy as it may seem. Business owners routinely buy copy without a full understanding of what it means to utilize and implement copy. Many do not understand how proper implementation can give them a return on their investment. Lack of proper implementation or even simply lack of implementation when it comes to copy is a *waste*.

Here is an example of a failure in regards to copy:

I was trying to connect with a high-profile client of Dan Kennedy. I had never been able to get more than an hour on the phone with him and I was *desperate* to get in contact. I called and asked if he was coming to the InfoSummit Conference in Baltimore, Maryland. Knowing that he would be much too busy to talk at the conference, I asked if we could take the same train from Boston to Baltimore so that I could sit with him and we could finally talk. He agreed and sent me his itinerary. I was living in Maryland at that time but I took the train up to Boston the day before in order to be able to take the train back to Maryland with this client the next day (pretty dedicated right!)

I finally got to meet him on the train and we started brainstorming some projects we could do together. Prior to the meeting, I had done some basic data work for him through Dan but we had never really done a larger scale, more meaningful project. That train ride, we started dreaming up an idea to promote his product through a national network of affiliates. We later met with Dan about our idea. We discussed strategy and concept. The deal was fleshed out and about a month later, we received binders full of copy for the project.

Unfortunately, the client had largely abandoned the idea and we had no use for the copy. NONE of it got executed. Some binders were never even opened. That story did not have a happy ending but your story can. If you are reading this book by Russell, then you are serious about copy. Working with him means you will receive copy that can convert your company's spectators into willing participants.

My name is Parthiv Shah and I own a company called eLaunchers.com. We are a digital marketing direct response agency in the business of implementing the core principles of digital and direct response marketing. We are the skilled technical labor that handles the logistics of copy beautification, data intelligence, campaign engineering, and deployment. Without a marketing production team, you may experience the *failure to launch* issue that I described in my earlier story. My company makes sure that you launch and then profit off your launch.

I typically work for two kinds of customers: professional practitioners and coaches/consultants/speakers. If you are the latter and have a "tribe," I offer an Ultimate Tribal Marketing Platform. My service develops a clear plan to target potential clients, provides the structures to implement that plan, and then tracks your results.

WHAT MAKES PERSUASIVE SALES COPY - PERSUASIVE

5 Step Implementation Plan for

Your Tribe is Your Legacy,
Let Us Help Your Build It.

Ultimate
TRIBAL MARKETING
Platform

Concept Visualization	Productization of the Deliverables	Technology Infrastructure	Sales, Marketing and JV Programs	Delivery and Logistics
• 1 1/2 day in person consult with Parthiv • Concept Mindmap & Everest diagram. • Study of 'Body of Knowledge' to identify content, systems and teachable talent. • Developing the core learning message. • Developing learning modality & content consumption plan. • Establish controls for time, data & money.	• Customer Value Journey & Customer Value Optimization • Lead magnet, trip-wire, core offer, profit maximizer & slack adjuster development. • Develop ascension, retention and content consumption props. • Welcome box, product binders/boxes and digital assets. • Weekly, monthly and event deliverables.	• Conversion Funnels and companion Infusionsoft Marketing Automation campaigns • Membership site for content delivery and learning management • Digital Asset library • Integration of webinar marketing to web • Event marketing • Tell-a-friend funnel and study buddy program • Implement time, data and money controls	• Traffic drivers: online & multi-step direct mail and email campaigns • Main sales letter with launch video or webinar • Tribal Shock and Awe • Automated email and phone follow up system • Down sell marketing & unconverted leads follow up program. • Affiliate recruitment system & customizable marketing resources • Result tracking system	• Integrate digital assets and data controls on membership site. • Automated production & distribution of binders, CDs, boxes & digital files. • Drip content and consumption campaigns • Event Marketing logistics • Appointment logistics • Customer service and fulfillment processes. • E-commerce and payment processing management

If you are a professional practitioner (dentist, orthodontist, clinician) or make money by appointment (attorney), then my Ultimate Conversion Concepts Platform is the best method of attack. The whole system only has eight facets to its implementation.

1. Develop a strategy for promoting business growth
2. Use InfusionSoft to implement our campaign designed just for your business
3. Develop funnels for your business
4. Impress your leads and clients
5. Use the copy to present your product to new leads
6. Send copy to handle rejection
7. Get your company referrals
8. Express gratitude

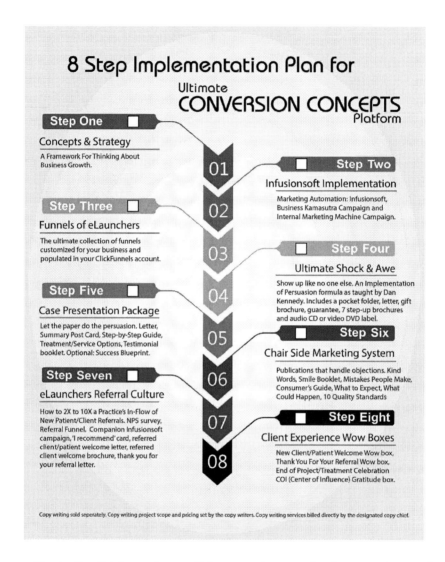

Typically, it takes a team of about twelve people about twelve weeks to complete a Conversion Concepts project. We go through a base camp with a little over 400 tasks and NONE of that includes copy. There is a mind-boggling amount of work that gets put into a project like this from *all* sides of production. Copy is a critical part of that process.

WHAT MAKES PERSUASIVE SALES COPY - PERSUASIVE

I wrote a book called *Business Kamasutra* which takes cues from an ancient Indian book called the *Kamasutra*. The *Kamasutra* was probably the first book ever written about human relationships. I drew upon the idea that finding prospects, making pitches, and closing deals were very similar to meeting, dating, and mating. My book draws parallels between business interactions and personal relationships. When I would talk to a new prospect about data science, data neurology, data intelligence and data driven decision making, they usually had a polite blank stare on their faces. I don't blame them because no one wants to have small talk about big data.

Dan Kennedy encouraged me to write my book several years ago but no one wanted to read a book called "Don't Waste Data." What started out as a hilarious conversation between me and my InfusionSoft representative back in 2013 turned into a book and an InfusionSoft campaign. My book uses the metaphor of "business is sex" to allow its readers to conceptualize business-prospect relations along with provide real steps for implementation in the reader's business. If you don't believe me, here is what Dan Kennedy has to say about *Business Kamasutra*:

> "Process Complexity is an extremely valuable asset. As the Kamasutra greatly complicates sex but gives its master dramatic advantage in sustaining the interest of his lover(s), the ability to implement this *Business Kamasutra gives* sustainable competitive advantage to a company."
> - Dan Kennedy

In India, arranged marriages are a common occurrence. In America, we have arranged business. The concepts of arranged marriage and arranged business are very similar as there is usually an usher connecting the two parties and establishing trust.

When starting a new relationship, you want to consider WHO you want to go after. That step is called *segmentation*. But in order to know who you want to date, you first need to know who YOU are. You will need to know WHO you like, WHAT pleases them, whether you are okay with doing the things they would like you to do, if you are you okay pleasing them that way, and the paycheck that comes with the wooing. If all of those criteria are met, then the journey towards the relationship becomes worth it.

If you do not do this right, then winning will be irrelevant and losing will be embarrassing.

Once you know who you are and who you want, you can organize, orchestrate, and execute an *approach*. In the marketing world, this is called traffic drivers. If the approach goes well, you will get *consent*. But be careful because the interesting thing about consent is that you must express gratitude and accept it immediately, otherwise the consent may get negated or watered down. Between *consent* and *mating*, there must be two very important steps in-between: trust and pleasure. You cannot gain pleasure without giving pleasure. Unless both parties trust each other and both are willing to take steps towards a relationship, you will never be able to turn your one night stand into a long-term relationship.

WHAT MAKES PERSUASIVE SALES COPY - PERSUASIVE

I turned this conversation, my book, and my philosophy about business relationships into an InfusionSoft campaign. What this campaign does is detail the specific steps to take during the "mating" process. The first step is driving traffic to the campaign specific landing page where you will acquire the lead and get them to schedule an appointment. On the day of the appointment, they will either attend and buy, attend and *not* buy, or not attend at all. We have a process in place to deal with what would happen in each of the three cases.

Once we get the client, the next step is to ask them how they feel about you. If they are very pleased to be working with you, show them some gratitude immediately. Send things that they can pass on to their friends. When you receive a referral, they are selling you to themselves in their own words which **deepens the bond in the relationship**. And anyone who gives you a referral is likely to not leave you because the number one rule of marketing is that he/she who is ascending is *not* descending.

Business Kamasutra Infusionsoft Campaign

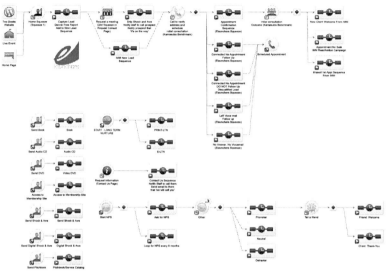

Now, I am going to give you the biggest gift I can give to anybody as a marketing automation expert. I am going to talk about THE TOOL that makes me more money than the rest of my war chest combined. It is using the phone for fail-safe follow-up.

My gift to you is this: I will write you a voicemail phone script when pitching to prospects AND I will write you a phone script for first time introductions.

When we meet for an hour, I will go through my process. I have an InfusionSoft campaign and a fail-safe follow up ritual along with a process to talk to prospects, establish trust, make opportunities, and turn those opportunities into projects. Now, you don't NEED InfusionSoft to implement this. Frankly, you don't need anything to do this. Technically, you could do it using a deck of index cards and some colorful tabs. *It is not about the sophistication of a system but it is about having a system in*

WHAT MAKES PERSUASIVE SALES COPY – PERSUASIVE

the first place. I have used index cards, three-ring binders, Salesforce.com, Sugar CRM, Goldmine, ACT, Sage, and a huge number of other services.

To do what I do to win, you don't *really* need anything. You just need to think like a system engineer and have processes in place for EVERYTHING. A system is nothing but a bunch of processes put together and a process is nothing but a bunch of rituals that are now documented.

If you want to accept my gift, go to: telephonefollowupsystem.com. Log in to the page, watch some videos, and then use the link to schedule an appointment. I will meet with you. We will talk about you, your leads, your follow-ups, and see what we can do to help you. If you have a lot of "diamonds in your database" or unconverted leads/prospects, we will work to get you a second date with those people who like you but don't buy.

We will help you make the secret fortune you were not aware you had.

If you have questions, reach out to me pshah@launchers.com or phone my office at 310-760-3953.

A MESSAGE FOR YOU FROM THE AUTHOR...

Even looking at this book means you are interested in growing your business.
And that makes you an exceptional business owner.
Congratulations!

WHO IS RUSSELL MARTINO??

Personally, I am a son. Brother. Husband. Father. Grandfather. Friend. Dog lover. Classical guitar player. Reader. Writer. Swimmer. And a guy happy to feed stray cats every now and then.

Professionally, I'm a direct-response copywriter and a direct marketing expert who measures success by the only thing that matters, which is results.

I'm married to the love of my life and have been for 32 years. We have daughters, grandkids and now

WHAT MAKES PERSUASIVE SALES COPY – PERSUASIVE

three great grandkids. *As you can imagine, there's never a dull moment!*

I grew up in an entrepreneurial household and learned early in life that it's not what you say that counts... it's what you do.

Since 1975, I have owned and/or played a key entrepreneurial role in building a variety of businesses, most of which did, and continue to do, remarkably well.

I've been helping business owners earn fortunes for over 25-years.

My marketing strategies and sales letters have generated well over a hundred million dollars in sales for my clients. Some have become bonified cash-in-the-bank millionaires entirely on the strength of my marketing and copywriting work. *This is not even a slight exaggeration.*

I actively write complete sales presentations, order pages and email traffic drivers in the most competitive copywriting niche in the world, the financial newsletter and financial services niche.

I was mentored into financial copywriting by, *(and continue to work with),* one of the greatest copywriters in the history of print, Clayton Makepeace.

(If you don't know who Clayton is Google him.)

If the idea of *at the least* doubling your sales is exciting to you, and you'd like to see it happen SOONER rather than LATER, maybe we should talk.

As a direct marketing expert, I may advise you on strategies to;

- Attract more new prospects and build your list;
- Systematically sell more of your product or service;
- Develop new products or services to generate whole new revenue streams;
- Take steps to gain a dominant competitive advantage in your market;
- Turn an underperforming business into an unstoppable sales machine;

- Increase the average transaction value of a purchase;
- Increase the frequency of purchase;
- Identify and take advantage of unrecognized opportunity to make sales;
- Develop new sales channels;
- Turn your business into a well-oiled profit making machine you love.

Besides being a master copywriter who can sell anything in print, *(the more expensive the better),* I design and write copy for COMPLETE EVERGREEN SELLING SYSTEMS that can generate endless leads and sell your product or service 24-hours a day, 365 days a year.

A small sample of the kind of results my copywriting/marketing work has produced includes;

- A 4-page special report that generated over $2 million in fees for a Houston law firm.
- A 2-page letter and a 17-minute video mailed to 68 people that generated over $1 million in sales for another client over seven months.
- A full page ad in the Houston Chronicle that brought in over $200,000 in cash business for a local Chiropractor over about 14 weeks... and kept his practice full for five years.
- The sales strategy and copy that secured $3.5 million in capital for my client in 8-weeks.
- Sales strategy and copy that has generated over $30 million in investment capital in small private placement projects for several different clients.
- A letter mailed to 371 people that generated over $100k in sales in a single afternoon and $125,000 more the following week for a small boutique furniture store.

WHAT MAKES PERSUASIVE SALES COPY – PERSUASIVE

- A lead generation piece that added over 80,000 people to my client's prospect list and produced over $120,000 in sales for a $97 front-end offer over a few months.
- A 16-page direct response sales letter that generates over $250,000 a MONTH in sales – and has been doing that now for eighteen straight months and counting.
- And on... and on.

WHY SHOULD YOU CARE?

Unless you want to sell a LOT MORE of your product or service, you shouldn't care at all.

But if you do want to sell a LOT MORE – this is important to know, because...

THE STRONGER YOUR COPY THE MORE YOU SELL

Having a strong sales message to engage your prospects, answer questions, handle objections and get them thrilled about doing business with you – before you ever hear from them...

...Is the ONLY THING I know of that can give you MAXIMUM RETURN for all the time, money, blood, sweat and tears you pour into your business.

You can reach Russell Martino by Email at: Russell@ConquestCopywriter.com or leave a message anytime 24-hours a day at: 281-487-5876.

$500 VALUE

SALES LETTER COPY CRITIQUE
LITTLE HINGES SWING BIG DOORS

FOLLOW THE INSTRUCTIONS BELOW TO CLAIM YOUR UP-TO 30-MINUTE SALES LETTER CRITIQUE WITH MASTER COPYWRITER & DIRECT MARKETING EXPERT RUSSELL MARTINO.

To claim your Sales Letter Copy Critique (delivered verbally), contact me through my Web site www.ConquestCopyWriter.com. Or contact me through my 24-hour message center at 281-487-5876.

Reference this Certificate and I will review one (1) sales letter or sales funnel. And give you *up to a 30-minute verbal critique* on how to make your message INSTANTLY more persuasive – so you convert more lookers into buyers – and sell more of your product or service without increased costs.

I will review your headline, sales-logic, bullet-points, offer, and more.

If time remains after your copy critique, you may ask any question about copywriting, direct marketing, fast-cash generation promotions, lead generation, traffic, conversion, evergreen selling systems, internal marketing, funnels, email marketing, print or radio advertising, direct mail, postcard advertising, and so on.

This REAL $500 value may result in higher conversion rates, more sales and greater profit practically overnight

**RUSSELL MARTINO
CONQUESTCOPYWRTING.COM**

$500 VALUE

WEB SITE CRITIQUE – FOR GREATER CLARITY ENGAGEMENT & PERSUASIVE IMPACT RESULTING IN MORE SALES...

Follow the Instructions below to Claim Your *Up-To 30-Minute* Web Site Critique With Master Copywriter & Direct Marketing Expert Russell Martino.

To claim your Web Site Critique, contact me through my Web site www.ConquestCopyWriter.com. Or contact me through my 24-hour message center at 281-487-5876.

Reference this Certificate and I will review your Web site for clarity, engagement and persuasive impact. And give you *up to a 30-minute verbal critique* on how to make your site INSTANTLY more persuasive – so can sell more of your product or service without increased costs.

After your site critique, *if time remains*, we can discuss ways to ramp up sales fast, and potentially double or triple your sales revenue. You may ask any question on copywriting, direct marketing, fast-cash promotions, lead generation, evergreen selling systems, internal marketing, funnels, email marketing, print advertising, radio, direct mail, and so on.

This REAL $500 value may result in higher conversion rates, more sales and greater profit, practically overnight.

RUSSELL MARTINO
CONQUESTCOPYWRTING.COM